AF600559

THE CATHOLIC UNIVERSITY OF AMERICA
CANON LAW STUDIES
No. 179

THE CANONICAL ERECTION OF RELIGIOUS HOUSES

AN HISTORICAL SYNOPSIS AND COMMENTARY

by

BERNARD JOSEPH FLANAGAN, A.B., S.T.L., J.C.L.
Priest of the Diocese of Burlington

A DISSERTATION

Submitted to the Faculty of the School of Canon Law of the Catholic University of America in Partial Fulfillment of the Requirements for the Degree of Doctor of Canon Law

THE CATHOLIC UNIVERSITY OF AMERICA PRESS
WASHINGTON, D. C.
1943

Nihil Obstat:

Hieronymus D. Hannan, S.T.D., J.C.D.,
Censor Deputatus.
Washingtonii, D. C., die 6 maii, 1943.

Imprimatur:

Matthaeus F. Brady, D.D.,
Episcopus Burlingtonensis.
Burlingtonii, die 6 maii, 1943.

Printed by
The Paulist Press
New York, N. Y.
51

TO

MY FATHER

AND

MOTHER

TABLE OF CONTENTS

CHAPTER IV

CANONICAL COMMENTARY

CHAPTER V

CHAPTER VI

CHAPTER VII

FOREWORD

THE purpose of the present work is twofold: to trace in summary form the development of the legislation on the canonical erection of religious houses from its origin down to the adoption of the New Code, and to present a canonical commentary on this legislation as it exists today. No attempt is made to analyze the constitutions of individual religious institutes or to discuss particular privileges which may have been granted to them in the matter of erecting religious houses. Both the historical and the canonical study are confined to a treatment of the general legislation which is pertinent to the subject.

The establishment of new religious houses is a natural consequence of the normal growth and expansion which is common to all religious institutes. However, it is an act in which the religious institute is not the only party concerned; local ordinaries and the faithful, both lay and clerical, are also affected by the erection of a new religious foundation. The legislative enactments of the Church, relative to the erection of religious houses, have always emphasized this fact, and the history of the legislation reveals an ever-present effort to provide for a natural and controlled expansion of religious institutes, while, at the same time, to safeguard the rights of local ordinaries and their dioceses. The subject-matter of this legislation is, therefore, of equal importance and interest to religious superiors and local ordinaries.

The first part of this work, the historical summary, is not intended to be an exhaustive presentation of all pre-Code legislation and doctrine on the erection of religious houses. An effort is made, however, to summarize the salient points of general legislation which effected important changes or developments in the status of the legal institute in question. The historical synopsis proceeds according to a fourfold chronological division, concurrent with the four periods during which legislation pertinent to the erection of religious houses was enacted. The sources of legislation which mark the boundaries of this fourfold division are: the Council of Chalcedon (451), the Decretal Collections of the thirteenth century, the Council of Trent (1545-1563) and the constitutional legislation of Pope Leo XIII (1878-1903).

It is important to note, in connection with the historical summary, that the term *domus religiosa* had a much wider connotation in pre-Code law than it has in the present discipline. The term was used in a generic sense as synonymous with an ecclesiastical foundation. In a more specific sense it was applied to houses which were set aside by episcopal authority, but without any sacramental blessing or consecration, for works of piety and charity. Monasteries, colleges, hospitals, orphanages and similar institutions were embraced by the term *domus religiosa,* employed in this more proper and restricted sense.[1] The legislation which is pertinent to the subject of this dissertation included all institutions of this type, that is, monasteries, colleges, hospitals, etc., in which there was an observance of regular discipline by a religious institute.

The second part of the dissertation is devoted to a canonical commentary on the present discipline of the Code relative to the erection of religious houses. This discipline is set forth in canons 495, 496 and 497. The legal order of the Code does not adapt itself to a logical and clear exposition of these canons. For purposes of clarity, therefore, and to avoid noxious repetitions, an effort has been made to systematize the principles enunciated in these three canons and to treat them in a logical order rather than in their numerical or legal sequence.

It should be clearly understood that the question for discussion does not concern the opening of the first house of a newly established religious institute. This would be identical with the erection of the institute and would be governed by the same formalities as the establishment of the institute itself.

The writer takes occasion to express his gratitude to His Excellency, the Most Reverend Matthew F. Brady, Bishop of Burlington, for the opportunity to pursue advanced studies. He is also sincerely thankful for the guidance and direction given him by the Faculty of the School of Canon Law of the Catholic University of America.

1 Cajetanus, *Iuris Canonici Universi Commentarius* (3 vols. Monachii, 1705), lib. III, tit. 36, n. 1.

Historical Synopsis

CHAPTER I

FIRST TO THIRTEENTH CENTURY

Article 1. Early Ages of the Church

It cannot be certainly affirmed from historical documents that there existed a complete and perfect religious state, to which the religious were bound by three vows, until the middle of the third century.[1] The first and most primitive form of true religious life was anchoretic monasticism, which had its origin in the Egyptian deserts, to which many of the devout faithful had fled, in order to escape the persecution of the Emperor Decius (249-251).[2] Although cenobitic monasticism, with its feature of life in common, soon arose from the earlier anchoretic practices, there is no evidence that there existed any juridical distinction for those who had embraced the religious life during these years of formative development. Religious remained subject to the local bishop in the same manner as the rest of the faithful and were entirely subject to his jurisdiction.[3] The erection of monasteries during this early period seems to have been accomplished with nothing more than a certain tacit approval of the local bishop.[4] There is no record of any legislation requiring his consent.

[1] Thomassinus, *Vetus et Nova Ecclesiae Disciplina circa Beneficia et Beneficiarios* (10 vols., Moguntiae, 1787), lib. III, pars I, cap. 12, n. 10.

[2] Wernz, *Ius Decretalium ad usum Praelectionum in Scholis Textus Iuris Canonici sive Iuris Decretalium*, III (2. ed., Romae, 1908), n. 602. (Hereafter this work is cited as *Ius Decretalium*). Cf. also, Eusebius Hieronymus, *Vita S. Pauli Eremitae*—Migne, *Patrologiae Cursus Completus, Series Latina* (Parisiis, 1844-1864), XXIII, 17.

[3] Steiger, "De Propagatione et Diffusione Vitae Religiosae,"—*Periodica de Re Canonica et Morali Utili praesertim Religiosis et Missionariis*, XIII (1924), (48). (Hereafter this periodical will be cited as *Periodica*.)

[4] Schmalzgrueber, *Ius Ecclesiasticum Universum* (5 vols. in 12, Romae, 1843-1845), lib. III, tit. 36, n. 28; Wernz, *Ius Decretalium*, III, n. 616.

The Council of Chalcedon, which was convened in the year 451, may be considered as the source of the first general legislation on the erection of religious houses. It is evident from the historical background of this Council and from the circumstances which attended it that clarification of the juridical relationship of religious to the local bishop had become most necessary. When the period of persecution came to an end in the fourth century, the monks began to come forth from the remote and desert places, where they had hitherto resided, and to settle in the towns and cities. Contact with the worldly life of the urban centers served to diminish the spirit of fervor which had characterized the monks of the earlier period. This factor, together with the lack of adequate supervision over the religious life, soon gave rise to serious disturbances of the good order of both Church and State. Undoubtedly the majority of the monks were zealous and sincere religious, but it is apparent that in a state of unorganization, which permitted anyone who so desired it to put on a religious garb and live according to his own notions of the religious life, there was much chance for abuse. Many of those who pretended to be religious were little more than charlatans, wandering about from place to place and living upon alms received from the pious faithful under false pretenses.[5]

Even more serious were the abuses which arose from the indiscreet part played by the monks of the Eastern Church in the violent dissension provoked by the heresy of Eutychianism. The fanaticism of these followers of the monk Eutyches, and their insolent conduct toward episcopal authority, had done grave harm to the cause of Christian unity during the years just previous to the Council of Chalcedon.[6]

It was undoubtedly for the purpose of remedying these abuses, by the provision of more strict external control over the religious life, that the Emperor Marcian (450-457) presented a petition to the Fathers of the Council, requesting that they forbid the erection of monasteries without the consent of the local bishop.[7]

[5] Butler, "Monasticism,"—*Cambridge Medieval History,* I (New York, 1911), p. 530.

[6] Chapman, *The Catholic Encyclopedia,* s. v. "Eutyches."

[7] *Allocutio Marciani,* cap. I—Mansi, *Sacrorum Conciliorum Nova et*

The Council acted favorably upon the request of the Emperor and enacted a decree whereby religious were forbidden to erect a monastery without the consent of their local bishop.[8] Since the Council of Chalcedon was a general council of the Church, this legislation had the force of general law. Subsequently it became the law of the civil realm also, when Justinian incorporated it in his *Novellae*.[9]

Article 2. Particular Councils From the Sixth to the Thirteenth Century

The acceptance of the legislation of the Council of Chalcedon as the universal law of the Church is witnessed by its repetition in the enactments of other councils during the succeeding centuries. Thus the Councils of Agde (506),[10] Orleans (511),[11] Epaon (518),[12] Lerida (524),[13] Barcelona (540),[14] and Toledo (694)[15] enacted decrees which repeated substantially the legislation of the Council of Chalcedon.

It is evident that there was no substantial change or development in the legislation pertinent to the erection of religious houses for seven hundred years after the Council of Chalcedon; for when Gratian compiled his famous *Concordia Discordantium Canonum* in the middle of the twelfth century he quoted the canon of the Council of Chalcedon as the still prevailing discipline.[16]

Amplissima Collectio (Paris, Arnhem, Leipzig, 1901-1927), VII, 174. (Hereafter this work is cited as Mansi.)

[8] Tit. 27, can. 4—Mansi, VII, 394.

[9] Nov. (5, 1).

[10] Can. 27—Mansi, VIII, 329.

[11] Can. 22—Mansi, VIII, 355.

[12] Can. 10—Mansi, VIII, 560.

[13] Can. 3—Mansi, VIII, 613.

[14] Can. 10—Mansi, IX, 109.

[15] Can. 11—Mansi, XII, 105.

[16] C. 10, C. XVIII, q. 2.

CHAPTER II

THIRTEENTH TO SIXTEENTH CENTURY

ARTICLE 1. FOURTH LATERAN COUNCIL (1215)

THE reforms of monastic life which originated at Cluny and Citeaux during the tenth and eleventh centuries brought a new plan of organization into the religious life. Whereas monasteries had previously been separate units, independent one from another, they now began to organize themselves into monastic congregations. This change in the form of government and organization resulted in the expansion of the same religious institute throughout several dioceses and made it difficult for the proper bishop to exercise his rightful authority and vigilance over it.[1]

During the twelfth century there rose up several heretical movements which, under the inspiration of a misguided and disordinate zeal, took the form of a mode of life patterned after that of the religious state. Some of these sects, such as that of the Waldensians, for example, became so strong that individual bishops were unable to cope with the evil or to prevent its spread. The situation called for stern and immediate action to avert this rising tide of heresy and to provide uniform regulations for those who wished to embrace the religious life.[2]

These circumstances as well as the changed conditions in the structure and organization of religious institutes, mentioned in the preceding paragraph, were undoubtedly the motivating cause of a decree which Innocent III (1198-1216) promulgated in the IV General Council of the Lateran (1215), whereby he reserved the right to establish religious institutes to the Holy See, and declared that

[1] Augustine, *A Commentary on the Code of Canon Law*, III, *Religious and Laymen* (5. ed., St. Louis: Herder, 1938), p. 8.

[2] Orth, *The Approbation of Religious Institutes*, The Catholic University of America Canon Law Studies, n. 71 (Washington, D. C.: The Catholic University of America, 1931), p. 29.

anyone who wished to found a new religious house must embrace the rule of one of the already approved institutes.[3]

Although this legislation was primarily intended to regulate the foundation of religious institutes, it also affected the law on the erection of religious houses. The enactment of the Council of Chalcedon still remained in force to the extent that the permission of the local bishop was sufficient and necessary for the erection of a religious house by an approved and established institute; but the former law was derogated in the measure that bishops could no longer approve the founding of a new religious house if it meant at the same time the establishment of an institute.

Article 2. Second General Council of Lyons (1274)

The II General Council of Lyons (1274) found it necessary to repeat the legislation of the IV General Council of the Lateran (1215) in more emphatic terms and to add further restrictions concerning the erection of religious houses. The astounding growth of the new and powerful mendicant orders during the intervening years had evidently given the Holy See some cause for concern.[4] Consequently the Council of Lyons made further efforts to provide more centralized control over the religious life by decreeing that those mendicant orders which had been founded since 1215, the year of the IV Lateran Council, could not erect new houses without the approval of the Holy See.[5]

The Franciscans, Dominicans, Carmelites and Augustinians, who had been founded during this era, but had obtained special approbation of the Holy See, were not included in this prohibition.[6]

[3] Can. 13—Mansi, XXII, 1002. This canon was later incorporated into the Decretals of Gregory IX—C. 9, X, *de religiosis domibus,* III, 36.

[4] Orth, *The Approbation of Religious Institutes,* p. 31.

[5] *Constitutiones a Gregorio X in Concilio Lugdunensi Generali Sancitae,* tit. 23, *de religiosis domibus*—Mansi, XXIV, 96. This canon was incorporated into the decretals of Boniface VIII—C. unic., *de religiosis domibus,* III, 17, in VI°.

[6] Schaefer, *Compendium de Religiosis ad Normam Codicis Iuris Canonici* (2. ed., Muenster i. W.: Libr. Aschendorff, 1931), n. 64, p. 101.

Article 3. Decretals of Boniface VIII (1294-1303)

The Decretals of Boniface VIII, promulgated in 1298, effected a further development in the legislation relative to the erection of religious houses. The privileges which Gregory X (1271-1276) had granted to certain mendicant institutes were revoked, and it was decreed that thenceforth no mendicant institutes whatever could erect a new house without special permission of the Holy See.[7] The Augustinians, however, were exempted by Pope Boniface from the observance of this legislation and continued to enjoy their privilege of erecting religious houses without seeking papal approbation.

It is clear from the text of this decretal that it referred solely to the strictly mendicant institutes—those orders which according to their rule could not own temporal goods. The monks of these institutes had to depend solely upon the alms of the faithful for their sustenance, and the public good demanded that there should not be too many of these communities in any one city or town.

This decree marked another step in the ever-increasing efforts of the Holy See to control the number of mendicant foundations and to prevent the dangers which might easily arise from an unrestricted expansion.[8]

Article 4. The *Clementinae*

The law enacted by the Decretals of Boniface VIII was confirmed by its repetition in the *Clementinae,* the authentic collection compiled under Pope Clement V (1305-1314) and promulgated by his successor, John XXII (1316-1334), in 1317. The Council of Vienne (1311-1312) had added the sanction of excommunication to the law of Pope Boniface, and the decree stating this canonical penalty was embodied in the *Clementinae.* It declared

[7] "Quum ex eo quod Praedicatores, Minores et religiosi alii mendicantes, in civitatibus, castris, villis, aut aliis locis ad inhabitandum domos vel loca suscipiunt, . . . hoc perpetuo edicto, ne deinceps aliquis vel aliqui de praedictis, . . . loca quaecumque de novo recipere . . . praesumant absque Sedis Apostolicae licentia speciali, plenam et expressam faciente de prohibitione huius modi mentionem; si secus egerint irritum decernentes."—C. I, *de excessibus Praelatorum,* V, 6, in VI°.

that any mendicant religious who presumed to erect a house without the permission of the Holy See would incur *ipso facto* excommunication.[8]

This remained the common law legislation until the time of the Council of Trent which opened in 1545. The non-mendicant religious and nuns, in conformity with the law of the Council of Chalcedon, still required only the permission of the local ordinary to erect a religious house, but the mendicant orders, with the exception of the Augustinians, had to obtain papal approbation as well, under pain of excommunication.

[8] C. 3, *de poenis,* V, 8, in Clem.

CHAPTER III

THE COUNCIL OF TRENT (1545-1563) TO LEO XIII (1878-1903)

ARTICLE 1. LEGISLATION CONCERNING REQUISITE PERMISSION

A. The Council of Trent

THE Council of Trent (1545-1563) enacted legislation regarding the erection of religious houses which was destined to be the source of much controversy during the next three centuries. The decree promulgated by the Council decreed that the permission of the local bishop was required for the erection of a religious house by any institute whatsoever.[1]

It was evident from the text of the decree that it applied to all religious institutes of regular observance. However, the fact that only episcopal permission was expressly mentioned gave rise to a difference of opinion concerning the status of the former law. The majority of canonists contended that the Tridentine decree did not abrogate the former legislation, but merely added another requisite beyond that of obtaining papal approbation, namely, the permission of the local ordinary.[2]

Fagnanus (1598-1678) was the chief authority for a contrary opinion, which held that the decree of the Council of Trent effected a change in the old law and made it unnecessary for any institute, except the Friars Minor and the Capuchins, to seek the approval

[1] ". . . nec de caetero similia loca sine episcopi in cuius dioecesi erigenda sunt, licentia prius obtenta."—Sess. XXV, *de regularibus*, c. 3.

[2] Barbosa, *Collectanea Doctorum in varia Concilii Tridentini Decreta et Canones* (Lugduni, 1657), Sess. XXV, *de regular. et monial.*, cap. 3, n. 28; Alteserra, *Asceticon sive Originum Rei Monasticae* (Neapoli, 1777), lib. IX, cap. 2; De Luca, *Il Dottore Volgare* (15 vols., Romae, 1673), lib. XIV, cap. 7, n. 1.

of the Holy See for the establishment of a religious house.[3] This argument was based on a literal interpretation of the texts involved in the legislation. It contended that the law of the Decretals applied only to the mendicant institutes, and that, since the Council of Trent had given the right of owning property to all these institutes, the Friars Minor and the Capuchins only being excepted,[4] they were no longer held by the decree of Pope Boniface.

In the years which immediately followed the Council of Trent there were numerous and repeated instances of recourse to the Holy See for permission to erect religious houses. Pius V (1566-1572), Gregory XIII (1572-1585) and Sixtus V (1585-1590) granted several permissions to various religious institutes which desired to establish religious houses.[5] This practice would seem to give support to the opinion which held that the permission of the Holy See was still necessary for the erection of religious houses, and it certainly indicates that in the mind of the legislator nothing had been detracted from the former law requiring papal approbation.

B. The Constitution "Instaurandae"

In 1652, Pope Innocent X (1644-1655) published the Constitution *"Instaurandae."*[6] The primary purpose of this legislation was the suppression of numerous small religious communities which had sprung up in Italy during the years after the Council of Trent. The impossibility of observing the norms of religious life and discipline in these small houses had given rise to serious abuses. In order to provide a remedy for the situation, the Pope forbade the erection of religious houses by any institute of regular observance without the permission of the Holy See.

[3] *Commentarium in Librum Decretalium* (3 vols., Venetiis, 1709), lib. III, *de institutionibus*, cap. *non amplius*, n. 55; cf. also Bouix, *De Iure Regularium* (3. ed., 2 vols., Parisiis, 1882), tom. I, pars II, sect. 2, cap. 1, § 4.

[4] Sess. XXV, *de regularibus*, c. 3.

[5] Cf. "Maisons Religieuses,"—*Analecta Iuris Pontificii*, IV (1860), 1823 sqq.

[6] 15 oct. 1652—*Codicis Iuris Canonici Fontes cura Emi. Petri Card. Gasparri editi*, 9 vols. (Romae, later Civitate Vaticana: Typis Polyglottis Vaticanis, 1923-1939) (Vols. VII-IX *ed. cura et studio Emi. Iustiniani Card. Serédi*), n. 233. (Hereafter this work is cited *Fontes*.)

The fact that Pope Innocent judged this legislation necessary seems to indicate that religious houses were being erected solely on the authorization of the local ordinary. His intention, therefore, was evidently to make clear that episcopal consent was not sufficient for the canonical erection of a religious house. However, the new legislation did not settle the controversy which had been occasioned by the decree of the Council of Trent. It was still not clear, at least in the opinion of canonists, whether or not papal approbation was necessary for the canonical establishment of all religious houses. The reason for this Constitution's lack to clarify the legal situation relative to the authorization required for the erection of religious houses was that the Pontiff had stated in the text of his document that he intended to provide a norm for institutes outside of Italy and the adjacent islands at a future date.[7] Death intervened, however, before the Pontiff could carry out his design.

It was now certain that papal approbation was necessary to erect a religious house of male regulars within the confines of Italy and its adjoining islands, but the status of the law outside these limits and with regard to women religious continued to be a source of canonical controversy.

Fagnanus, as a logical deduction from his opinion interpreting the decree of the Council of Trent, contended that outside of Italy and its adjacent islands all religious, with the exception of the Friars Minor and the Capuchins, could still erect houses with the sole permission of the local ordinary.[8] As Secretary of the Sacred Congregation of Bishops and Regulars, Fagnanus was the principal compiler of the Constitution *"Instaurandae."*[9] Hence a great deal of authority was attached to his opinion that this legislation applied only to male regulars within the territorial limits of Italy and its adjacent islands. This opinion was also supported by such

[7] § 5: "Intendimus autem in praemissis etiam ultra Italiam et insulae adiacentes, prout expedire volumus, providere."—*Fontes,* n. 233.

[8] *Commentarium in Librum Decretalium,* lib. I, *de officio iudicis ordinarii,* cap. *grave,* n. 53.

[9] Bouix, *De Iure Regularium,* tom. I, pars II, sect. 2, cap. 1.

eminent canonists as Pignatelli (1600-1675),[10] Engel (1634-1674),[11] Reiffenstuel (1641-1703)[12] and Bouix (1808-1870).[13]

Canonists of equal authority, however, contended that even outside of Italy and the adjacent islands the permission of both the Holy See and the local ordinary was required. Among these authors were De Luca (1614-1683),[14] Schmalzgrueber (1663-1735),[15] Pichler (1670-1736),[16] Devoti (1744-1820)[17] and Ferraris (1687-1763).[18] The chief proponent of this opinion, however, was Pope Benedict XIV (1740-1758). Writing in the middle of the eighteenth century, the noted Pontiff and canonist declared that in his time it was not only the common opinion, but the accepted norm for practice in the Roman Tribunals, that institutes of regular observance could not erect a religious house in any part of Christendom without the permission of both papal and episcopal authority.[19]

It is evident from the text of various decisions handed down by the Roman Rota and the Sacred Congregation of Bishops and Regulars that even before this time it had become the practice of the Roman Curia to demand papal approbation for the erection of religious houses, even outside of Italy.[20]

[10] *Consultationes Canonicae* (11 vols. in 4, Coloniae Allobrogum, 1700), tom. X, consult. 91, n. 12 sqq.

[11] *Collegium Universum Iuris Canonici* (Venetiis, 1760), lib. III, tit. 36, n. 3.

[12] *Ius Canonicum Universum* (7 vols., Venetiis, 1735), lib. III, tit. 36, n. 28 sqq.

[13] *De Iure Regularium,* tom. I, pars II, sect. 2, cap. 1 sqq.

[14] *Il Dottore Volgare,* lib. XIV, pars II, cap. 7, n. 1 sqq.

[15] *Ius Ecclesiasticum Universum,* lib. III, tit. 36, nn. 28-30.

[16] *Epitome Iuris Canonici* (2 vols., Venetiis, 1755), tom. I, lib. III, tit. 36, n. 3.

[17] *Institutionum Canonicarum Libri IV* (2 vols., Leodii, 1860), tom. II, lib. II, tit. 10, n. 2.

[18] *Prompta Bibliotheca, Canonica, Iuridica, Moralis, Theologica, necnon Ascetica, Polemica, Rubricistica, Historica* (9 vols., Romae, 1885-1899), s. v. "conventus," art. 1, n. 38. (Hereafter this work is cited as *Bibliotheca.*)

[19] *De Synodo Dioecesana* (3 vols., Romae, 1788), tom. I, lib. IX, cap. I, n. 9.

[20] S. R. Rotae, *Toletanus manutentionis,* 7 febr. 1656—*Sacrae Rotae Romanae Decisiones Recentiores* (Romae, 1670), pars XII, p. 256; S. R. R., *Caesaraugustana fundationis,* 12 nov. 1657—*ibidem,* p. 578; S. R. R., *Eystet-*

Article 2. Legislation Restricting the Right of the Local Ordinary to Approve the Erection of a New Religious House

From the time of the Council of Trent the legislation on the erection of religious houses began to be more detailed in its enactments. Other legal requirements, besides that of the permission of legitimate authority, were introduced through the enactments of papal constitutions. The first of these constitutions, entitled "*Quoniam,*" was published by Clement VIII (1592-1605).[21] It decreed that the local ordinary must consult the superiors of other institutes already established in the vicinity, before permitting a new religious house to be erected.

Gregory XV (1621-1623) confirmed and amplified this legislation in the Constitution "*Cum alias.*"[22] This decree, in the same manner as that of Clement VIII, applied to all institutes of regular observance and prohibited the erection of religious houses by these orders, unless there were twelve religious assigned to live therein and this number could be suitably maintained from the revenues and customary alms of the locality. It further qualified the enactment of Clement VIII regarding the protection of the rights of neighboring communities, by demanding that the local ordinary consult the superiors of all religious houses within a distance of four thousand paces and obtain their consent to the new foundation, unless it was definitely clear to him that the interests of these existing communities would not be prejudiced. If there were no other monasteries in the neighborhood, the bishop was obliged to consult the inhabitants of the place and to inquire whether their

ten. fundationis, 27 iun. 1729—*Decisiones Sacrae Romanae Rotae coram Ratto* (Romae, 1752), tom. III, p. 179; S. C. Ep. et Reg., *Montis Regalis,* 21 apr. 1690—Ferraris, *Bibliotheca,* s. v. "conventus," art. 1, n. 7; S. C. Ep. et Reg., *in Atren. hospitii,* 31 aug. 1691—*Ibidem,* n. 9. Cf. also S. C. Ep. et Reg., *Romana,* 26 mart. 1841—*Fontes,* n. 1929.

[21] 23 iul. 1603—*Fontes,* n. 190.

[22] 27 aug. 1622—*Bullarum Diplomatum et Privilegiorum Sanctorum Romanorum Pontificum Taurinensis Editio* (25 vols., Augustae Taurinensis, 1857-1872), XII, 719. (Hereafter this work is cited as *Bullar. Roman. Taur.*)

alms would be sufficient to support a community of at least twelve religious.[23]

Canonists were not agreed as to the obligation of the bishop to consult the pastor of the place wherein the new house was to be located. Clement VIII had stated in his constitution that, in addition to the other institutes in the vicinity, the bishop should consult others whose interests were concerned.[24] It was the more common opinion among the authors that the pastor should be included in the number of those whose interests were involved, but the extent of his rights was a matter of controversy. Some authors held that the pastor should not only be consulted, but that his consent should be obtained.[25] Others supported the opinion that he should be consulted, but did not require his consent.[26] A third group contended that the bishop was not obliged even to consult the pastor when it was evident that parochial rights would not be injured.[27]

The controversy presented little practical difficulty, however, since the Constitution "*Cum alias*" had granted the right of appeal from the bishop's decision to all whose interests were prejudiced by it. The appeal was to be made to the Sacred Congregation of Bishops and Regulars and had suspensive effect.[28]

Article 3. Legislation Affecting the New Religious House Itself

In addition to the conditions affecting the bishop's right to approve the erection of a religious house, other legal requirements,

[23] Gregory XV, const. "*Cum alias,*" § 3—*Bullar. Roman. Taur.*, XII, 719.

[24] § 1: " . . . nisi vocatis et auditis . . . aliis interęsse habentibus . . . "—*Fontes*, n. 190.

[25] Cf. Pignatelli, *Consultationes Canonicae*, tom. I, consult. 179, n. 52; De Luca, *Il Dottore Volgare*, lib. XIV, cap. 7, n. 4; Schmalzgrueber, *Ius Ecclesiasticum Universum*, lib. III, tit. 36, n. 35.

[26] Petra, *Commentaria ad Constitutiones Apostolicas* (5 vols. in 2, Venetiis, 1729), tom. I, const. 2, sect. 1, n. 31; Reiffenstuel, *Ius Canonicum Universum*, lib. III, tit. 36, n. 33.

[27] Bouix, *De Iure Regularium*, tom. I, pars II, sect. 2, cap. 4; Bonal, *Institutiones Canonicae* (2 vols., Parisiis, Lugduni, 1898), II, p. 367.

[28] Const. "*Cum alias,*" § 4—*Bullar. Roman. Taur.*, XII, 719.

relating to the new foundation itself, were enacted by the Council of Trent and the papal constitutions issued during this period.

The Council of Trent decreed that only that number of religious could form a new religious house of any institute which could be adequately supported by the proper revenues of the foundation and the usual alms of the locality.[29]

Gregory XV, in the previously mentioned Constitution *"Cum alias,"* gave more specific legislation in this regard by decreeing that a new house could not be erected unless there were twelve members to form the community and this number could be suitably maintained.[30]

A decree of the Sacred Congregation of the Council, issued by order of Urban VIII (1623-1644),[31] confirmed the legislation of Gregory XV in this regard, but qualified it by a clause to the effect that if a house were erected without the legal number of members it would be subject to the visitation, correction and jurisdiction of the local bishop. From this time, therefore, a religious house could be erected without the legal number of twelve religious, but in the event of such an establishment the community lost all privileges of exemption from episcopal jurisdiction.[32]

In 1624 Urban VIII issued the Constitution *"Romanus Pontifex,"* in which he revoked all privileges which had been obtained by various institutes, permitting them to erect religious houses without the consent of the local ordinary.[33] At the same time the Pontiff imposed upon the superiors of all religious institutes the obligation of conforming to the norms established by the Council of Trent and the papal constitutions, under pain of excommunication and privation of office.

[29] Sess. XXV, *de regularibus,* c. 3.

[30] Const. *"Cum alias,"* § 1—*Bullar. Roman. Taur.,* XII, 719.

[31] S. C. C., decr., 21 iun. 1625—*Fontes,* n. 2460.

[32] A decree of the Sacred Congregation of the Propagation of the Faith, dated Jan. 30, 1627, declared that institutes in missionary countries were not bound by the legislation of Gregory XV and Urban VIII, which required each house to have twelve members—*Collectanea Sacrae Congregationis de Propaganda Fide* (2 vols., Romae, 1907), I, n. 32. (Hereafter this work is cited as *Coll. S. C. P. F.*)

[33] 28 aug. 1624—*Fontes,* n. 204.

Article 4. Monasteries of Nuns

The question as to whether the legislation enacted during this period applied to monasteries of nuns remained a subject of canonical controversy until the promulgation of the Code. Several authors held that the authorization of the Holy See was not required to erect a monastery of nuns, even within the confines of Italy.[34] This contention was based chiefly on the authority of Fagnanus and his interpretation of the Constitution *"Instaurandae"* as being extended only to institutes of male regulars within the confines of Italy and its adjoining islands. Bouix,[35] in summarizing the arguments relative to the subject, asserted that nuns were bound solely by the legislation of the Council of Trent in the matter of erecting religious houses, namely, that they required the approval of the local bishop and must have that number of religious which could be adequately supported by the revenues of the foundation and the usual alms of the locality.

The more common opinion, however, contended that the approbation of both the Holy See and the bishop was necessary in order that an institute of nuns could validly erect a monastery.[36] This opinion continued to prevail until the adoption of the New Code by reason of its acceptance as the norm for practice by the Roman Curia. Both Bouix and Fagnanus, chief protagonists of the contrary opinion, although asserting that their opinion was more correct in theory, admitted that it was the practice of the Sacred Congregation to refuse juridical recognition to monasteries of nuns, unless they had been established by express permission of the Holy See.[37] The truth of this admission is verified and borne out by

[34] Fagnanus, *Commentarium in Librum Decretalium,* lib. III, *de institutionibus,* cap. *amplius,* n. 55 sqq.; Monacelli, *Formularium Legale Practicum Fori Ecclesiastici* (4 vols. Romae, 1713), I, tit. VI, form. 19, adnot. 17; Bouix, *De Iure Regularium,* tom. I, pars II, sect. 2, cap. 36, qu. 1.

[35] *Loc. cit.*

[36] Ferraris, *Bibliotheca,* s. v. "conventus," art. 1, n. 31; De Luca, *Il Dottore Volgare,* lib. XIV, cap. 7, n. 9; Vecchiotti, *Institutiones Canonicae* (3 vols., 19. ed., Augustae Taurinorum, 1886), II, cap. 5, n. 4; Grandclaude, *Ius Canonicum iuxta Ordinem Decretalium* (3 vols., Parisiis, 1882), II, tit. 36, p. 472.

[37] Cf. Fagnanus, *Commentarium in Librum Decretalium,* lib. I, tit. *de*

various decisions of the Sacred Congregation of Bishops and Regulars during the four centuries which intervened between the Council of Trent and the promulgation of the Code.[38]

Hence, whatever the merits of the canonical dispute among the authors, there seems to have been no doubt concerning the mind of the Church: it was the consistent practice of the Holy See to require the same approval for the erection of new monasteries of nuns as for houses erected by male regulars. The Sacred Congregation was also equally insistent that the new monastery should have the legal number of twelve religious to form the community.[39]

The question as to the necessity of consulting the superiors of other religious houses in the locality was not so clear. Some authors held that this formality was required for the erection of monasteries of nuns on the grounds that the Constitutions *"Quoniam"* and *"Cum alias,"* which were the basis of this legislation, made no distinction between monasteries of men and of women.[40] Other canonists, however, distinguished between monasteries of nuns which were strictly mendicant and those which did not have to depend solely upon alms for their support. According to this opinion, the bishop was obliged to consult the superiors of other religious houses in the vicinity only when there was question of the erection of a monastery of mendicant nuns, since the purpose of the law ceased when a non-mendicant institute was involved.[41]

officio iudicis ordinarii, cap. *grave,* n. 53; Bouix, *De Iure Regularium,* tom. I, pars II, sect. 2, cap. 1.

[38] S. C. Ep. et Reg., *Amerina,* 8 nov. 1574—*Fontes,* n. 1315; *Vicentina,* 10 apr. 1615—*Fontes,* n. 1664; *Pacen.,* 1 mart. 1703—Bizzarri, *Collectanea in Usum Secretariae S. C. Episcoporum et Regularium* (2. ed., Romae, 1885), p. 337; (hereafter this work is cited as *Coll. S. C. Ep. et Reg.*); *Spoletana,* 18 dec. 1836—Bizzarri, *op. cit.,* p. 76; *Americana Votorum,* 2 sept. 1864.—Bizzarri, *op. cit.,* p. 723; *Sorana,* 20 iun. 1851—*Fontes,* n. 1960.

[39] Cf. S. C. Ep. et Reg., *Portugallien.,* 6 iun. 1605—Bizzarri, *op. cit.,* p. 334; *Ferrarien.,* 27 apr. 1855—Bizzarri, *op. cit.,* p. 637; cf. also Ferraris, *Bibliotheca,* s. v. "moniales," art. 2, nn. 5, 7, 9, 15 and 16.

[40] Thus, Donatus, *Rerum Regularium Praxis Resolutoria* (4 vols., Neapoli, 1652), tom. I, pars II, tract. I, n. 21; Barbosa, *Collectanea Doctorum in varia Concilii Tridentini Decreta et Canones,* Sess. XXV, *de regular. et monial.,* cap. 3, n. 29; Ferraris, *Bibliotheca,* s. v. "conventus," art. 1, n. 31.

[41] Schmalzgrueber, *Ius Ecclesiasticum Universum,* lib. III, tit. 36, n. 38;

A study of the texts of several decisions handed down by the Sacred Congregation of Bishops and Regulars reveals that the Holy See carefully investigated the financial status of a new foundation of women religious before granting approval to it. The house had to be free from debts and mortgages, and the dowries of the nuns had to be invested in property of a stable character. It was also required that the house be erected within the environs of a town or city, and that it be completely surrounded by a high wall in order to protect and safeguard the privacy of the cloister. When these conditions were fulfilled, the Sacred Congregation did not seem to concern itself with the question of consulting other institutes in the locality.[42]

Article 5. Religious Congregations

The great heresies of the sixteenth century, with their consequent defection of great bodies of people from the Faith, prompted the rise of a new form of religious life, dedicated to the works of the active ministry. The members of these institutes professed simple vows only, or, in some instances, took no vows at all, and devoted themselves, in accordance with their rule and purpose, to such varied works of the sacred ministry as the conduct of home and foreign missions, the care of the sick and the poor, and the giving of Christian instruction.[43]

There seems to have been no question, however, as to the status of the law with regard to the erection of houses by these institutes.

Pignatelli, *Consultationes Canonicae,* tom. I, consult. 179, n. 73; Monacelli, *Formularium Legale Practicum,* I, tit. VI, form. 19, nn. 18, 19.

[42] Cf. S. C. Ep. et Reg., *Sorana,* 20 iun. 1851—*Fontes,* n. 1960; *Amerina,* 8 nov. 1574—*Fontes,* n. 1315.

It may be noted, however, that a decision of the Sacred Congregation of the Council forbade the erection of monasteries of nuns contiguous to an existing monastery of male regulars; cf. S. C. C. *in Conchen.,* ? iul. 1586—Pallottini, *Collectio Omnium Conciliorum et Resolutionum quae in causis propositis apud Sacram Congregationem Cardinalium S. Concilii Tridentini Interpretum prodierunt ab eius institutione anno MDLXIV ad annum MDCCCLX distinctis titulis alphabetico ordine per materias digesta* (18 vols., Romae, 1868-1893), s. v. "moniales," § 1, n. 4.

[43] Schaefer, *De Religiosis,* n. 12.

The various legislative enactments up until this time had referred expressly only to the religious orders. It was the common opinion among canonists, therefore, that the institutes of simple vows required only the permission of the local ordinary in order to establish new foundations.[44]

[44] Bouix, *De Iure Regularium,* tom. I, pars II, sect. 2, cap. 1; Monacelli, *Formularium Legale Practicum,* I, tit. VI, form. 19, n. 11.

CHAPTER IV

LEO XIII (1878-1903) TO THE CODE (1918)

Article 1. The Constitution *"Romanos Pontifices"*

The chief development in the legislation during this period was the settlement of the controversy concerning the permission required to erect a religious house. In the Constitution *"Romanos Pontifices,"* [1] Leo XIII decreed that both papal and episcopal permission were necessary for the erection of a religious house by any institute of regular observance. The Constitution had application at first to England and Scotland, but later was extended to the United States by its acceptance and incorporation into the acts of the III Plenary Council of Baltimore (1884).[2]

Article 2. The Constitution *"Conditae a Christo"*

In 1900 Leo XIII published the celebrated Constitution *"Conditae a Christo."* [3] By this legislation institutes of simple vows were, for the first time, placed on a definite and clearly defined juridical basis. The distinction between congregations of pontifical approval and institutes of diocesan approval was established, and the relations between these institutes and the local ordinary were accurately defined.[4]

In the matter of erecting religious houses, the Constitution decreed that no institute of simple vows could establish a house without the express approval of the local ordinary. This was an application of the law of the Council of Trent to these institutes. It

[1] 8 maii 1881—*Fontes,* n. 582.

[2] *Acta et Decreta Concilii Plenarii Baltimorensis III* (1884) (Baltimorae, 1886), n. 89. The legislation was also repeated in the decrees of the Plenary Council of Latin America, held at Rome in 1899—*Acta et Decreta Concilii Americae Latinae* (Romae, 1902), n. 301.

[3] 8 dec. 1900—*Fontes,* n. 644.

[4] Cf. Larraona, "Commentarium Codicis,"—*Commentarium pro Religiosis,* I (1920), 171. (Hereafter this periodical will be cited *CpR.*)

was further decreed that an institute of diocesan approval could not establish a house in another diocese without obtaining the consent of the bishop of the place where the mother house was located and of the bishop in whose diocese the new house was to be erected.[5]

Article 3. The *Normae* of 1901

On the 28th of June, 1901, the Sacred Congregation of Bishops and Regulars issued the so-called *Normae* to which institutes of simple vows had to conform in order to receive pontifical approval.[6] Among the norms pertinent to the erection of religious houses were the following:

1. The erection of a new house was designated as a disciplinary matter which required the superior to obtain the favorable and decisive suffrage of the council.[7]
2. The express consent of both the local ordinary and the council of the institute was demanded.[8]
3. In places subject to the Sacred Congregation of the Propagation of the Faith, the consent of that Congregation was necessary for the erection of a religious house.[9]
4. The period of novitiate in institutes of pontifical right had to be observed in a house approved by the Sacred Congregation of Bishops and Regulars.[10]

Article 4. Further Legislative Enactments

In the years which immediately preceded the adoption of the Code two further acts of legislation relative to the erection of religious houses were issued from the Holy See. The first of these acts was a letter of the Sacred Congregation of the Propagation

[5] Const. "*Conditae a Christo,*" § 1, IV—*Fontes,* n. 644.

[6] *Normae secundum quas S. Congr. Episcoporum et Regularium procedere solet in approbandis novis Institutis votorum simplicium* (Romae: Typis S. C. de Prop. Fide, 1901). (Hereafter these norms are cited as the *Normae* of 1901.)

[7] *Normae* of 1901, art. 271.

[8] *Ibidem,* art. 305.

[9] *Ibidem,* art. 306.

[10] *Ibidem,* art. 76.

of the Faith in which bishops were instructed to observe the provisions of the Constitution "*Romanos Pontifices*" in their entirety, and to refrain from approving the erection of religious houses in territory subject to the jurisdiction of the Sacred Congregation of the Propagation of the Faith, without first obtaining the permission of that body.[11]

The final act of legislation was an instruction of the Sacred Congregation of the Religious, issued in 1909, which concerned the financial matters relative to the erection of a religious house.[12] This instruction declared that no religious house could be erected or altered unless the necessary money was at hand; no debt or other financial obligation could be contracted in order to accomplish the desired purpose.

[11] S. C. Prop. Fide, litt. encycl., 7 dec. 1901—*ASS,* XXIV (1901-1902), 639; *Fontes,* n. 4938.

[12] S. C. de Relig., instr., 30 iul. 1909, n. VIII—*AAS,* I (1909), 697; *Fontes,* n. 4394.

HISTORICAL SUMMARY

THE canonical legislation relative to the erection of religious houses had its origin in a canon promulgated by the Council of Chalcedon (451). Although the monastic state had been in existence for some two centuries previous, there is no evidence that, up until this time, any juridical distinction was made for those who had embraced the religious life. The decree of the Council of Chalcedon made religious subject to the local bishop and required them to obtain his consent in order to erect a religious house. This legislation was ratified by various particular councils in the following centuries and remained the common law of the Church until the thirteenth century.

The promulgation of the Decretals of Gregory IX and of Boniface VIII in the thirteenth century effected the first important change in the legislation on religious houses. In order to provide more centralized control over religious institutes, the right to approve new houses of mendicant orders was reserved to the Holy See. Only the Hermits of St. Augustine, by special concession, were exempted from this decree. Non-mendicant institutes were not affected by the legislation of the Decretals and continued to require only the permission of the local ordinary to erect a religious house.

The sixteenth and seventeenth centuries witnessed a further evolution of the legal institute in question through the enactments of the Council of Trent and various papal constitutions. Although these acts of legislation were in some respects characterized by a lack of clarity, which resulted in a controversy concerning certain practical aspects of the law, it was the common opinion of authors, as well as the accepted norm for the practice of the Roman Curia, that the permission of papal and episcopal authority was necessary to erect a house of any institute of regular observance. Various provisions for the protection of the rights of neighboring communities were also introduced during this period. Bishops were obliged to consult the superiors of other institutes within a distance of four thousand paces, if there was any danger that their interests would be prejudiced by the establishment of a new community within the region. The religious discipline and the financial security of the new foundation were also safeguarded by legislation demanding a legal number of twelve religious to form the new community, together with an assurance of sufficient income to support that number.

The Legislation of Leo XIII was notable for its definition of the juridical status of institutes of simple vows. The legislation of the Council of Trent relative to the erection of religious houses was extended to these institutes, and the local ordinary was given the exclusive right to approve the erection of religious houses by them. In places subject to the Sacred Congregation of the Propagation of the Faith, however, the permission of that body was required, and the erection of a novitiate by an institute of pontifical right was also decreed to be a matter requiring papal approbation.

Canonical Commentary

CHAPTER V

GENERAL NOTIONS

Article 1. The Religious House

A religious house is defined by the Code as the house of any religious institute in general.[1] The term has a much more restricted sense than it had in pre-Code law, for it is now a technical word which signifies only the house of a religious institute.[2] Hospitals, orphanages, schools and similar institutions, dedicated to works of piety and charity, which the former law included in the term *domus religiosa* are now generically designated by the Code as ecclesiastical institutes.[3]

The present discipline of the Code employs the term *religious house* in both a material and a formal sense. It uses the term in a material sense to indicate the place or edifice in which the religious reside and carry on their proper works. Thus, it states that superiors shall reside in their houses and not leave them except according to the norms of the constitutions; [4] it prescribes that the period of the novitiate be passed in a house of novices; [5] and it declares that the novitiate shall be separated from that part of the house in which

[1] Can. 488, 5°.

[2] Societies of men and women who live in community life, under the direction of legitimate superiors and according to approved constitutions, but who take no public vows, are not religious institutes in the proper sense (can. 673, § 1). However, the Code expressly states that in the matter of erecting religious houses these societies are to observe the same norms as religious congregations (can. 674). Therefore, accordingly as they are of diocesan or pontifical approval, clerical or lay, these societies will observe the norms of canons 495 and 497 which properly apply to them.

[3] Cf. cans. 1489 sqq.; 1544 sqq.

[4] Can. 508.

[5] Can. 555, § 1, 2°.

the professed religious reside.[6] But in its formal and proper sense the term designates the religious community, that is, the moral collegiate person which constitutes the smallest unit or social group of which religious institutes, according to the common law, are composed.[7] The term does not designate the community in the abstract, however, but rather in the concrete, as a particular religious community having its domicile in a definite and determinate place.[8]

From another aspect one may also distinguish a wide and a strict use of the term *religious house*. In the wide sense it is commonly used to describe any community of religious, or any residence inhabited by them. In the strict canonical sense, however, the term denotes a permanent and legitimately established foundation, where the religious practice the common life, in accordance with the constitutions of their institute and under the direction of their proper superiors.[9]

An analysis of this definition reveals that there are two inseparable elements involved in the concept of a true religious house: a distinct community with its proper superior, and a place legitimately set aside for the observance of the religious life according to the norms of approved constitutions. A house or residence used by religious or inhabited by them is not a religious house in the canonical sense unless it conforms to this concept. Hence, many types of religious buildings and dwellings are not true religious houses for the reason that they lack one or the other of these elements. Villas, for instance, farmhouses (*grangiae*) and other similar residences which are used primarily for secular purposes, are commonly excluded from

[6] Can. 564, § 1; cf. also, cans. 574, §§ 1-2; 599, § 1.

[7] A canonically erected house which has a community of at least three religious is a moral collegiate person; cf. page 27. Recognition of the juridical capacity of a religious house to act legally, to own property, etc., is had in cans. 531; 532, § 1; 536, § 1; 582, 1 °, and 594, § 2.

[8] Cf. Larraona, "Commentarium Codicis,"—*CpR*, III (1922), 47. The relationship between the religious community and its place of residence, which is effected by canonical erection, is so close that under certain circumstances a change of site involves a change of canonical personality and is equivalent to a new foundation. This matter is treated at greater length in Chapter X of this work.

[9] Pejška, *Ius Canonicum Religiosorum* (3. ed., Friburgi Brisgoviae: Herder, 1927), p. 49.

the classification of religious houses.[10] Ordinarily there is no observance of the customary religious life in these residences. The religious, therefore, are not considered to reside there *as religious*. These residences are mere secular dwellings and are not subject to the norms for the erection of a religious house.[11]

Likewise, residences of religious which have no legal status independent from that of the principal house to which they are attached are not religious houses in the proper sense. The concepts of community and superior are correlative notions. There can be no true community without an authority to govern it, and there can be no true superior without a proper community subject to him. Both of these notions are integral to the concept of a true religious house. Hence, any residence of religious in which there is lacking a community with legal existence, distinct and independent from that of another house, is not a religious house in the strict sense. The same is also true of a house which is presided over by a religious who is a mere delegate, revocable at will, of the superior of a more important community. These are merely filial houses or dependent residences and are considered in law as a part of the religious house upon which they depend.[12]

The Code of Canon Law does not expressly specify any particular number of religious as being necessary to constitute a distinct religious community. However, since canon 100, § 1, states that a minimum of three physical persons is necessary to constitute a collegiate moral person, it is evident that a group of less than three religious could have no legal status as a distinct moral person. Canonists who discuss the point commonly agree that the enjoyment of distinct moral personality is an essential condition for the constitu-

[10] Cf. Larraona, "Commentarium Codicis,"—*CpR*, III (1922), 48; Coronata, *Institutiones Iuris Canonici*, I (ed. altera, Taurini, 1939), n. 504; Pejška, *Ius Canonicum Religiosorum*, p. 49.

[11] It may be noted, however, that it is possible, in particular cases, for houses of this kind to be erected as true religious houses. Sometimes the residence may be used for religious as well as purely secular purposes. The character of the house, therefore, and the intention of the superiors in opening or erecting the building must be taken into consideration.

[12] Cf. can. 497, § 3; cf. also the article on filial houses, pp. 30 sqq., in this work.

tion of a true community and, therefore, of a true religious house.[13] Vermeersch (1858-1936), however, holds that even two religious can constitute a true juridical house, if the constitutions of an institute permit such foundations.[14] It is true that a residence inhabited by less than three religious could be erected as a non-collegiate ecclesiastical institute,[15] but, since the religious could have no legal status apart from a larger and principal community to which they are attached, it would lack that which appears to be an integral element of a true religious house, namely, the character of a distinct and independent community, enjoying its own moral personality before the law.

In order to avoid any misinterpretation of this point, however, it must be emphasized that a community of three religious is necessary only for the first formation or establishment of a religious house. If a house has been canonically erected, and then, through death or transfer of its members, becomes reduced to even one member, it retains its legal status.[16]

Another mark or quality which a true religious house must possess, in conformity to the definition given above, is that of stability. A legitimately established religious house is a moral person before the law and as such is by nature perpetual.[17] It cannot exist, therefore, except in a place where the religious community has a fixed and abiding residence. Hence, a group of religious who, by reason of war, persecution or accident, take up their residence in a place without the intention of establishing a domicile there, or at least of prolonging their sojourn, cannot constitute a juridical house.[18]

[13] Coronata, *Institutiones*, n. 504; Larraona, "Commentarium Codicis,"—*CpR*, III (1922), 48; Battandier, *Guide Canonique pour les Constitutions des Instituts à Voeux Simples* (6. ed., Paris, 1923), 422; Bastien, *Directoire Canonique à l'usage des Congrégation à Voeux Simples* (3. ed., Bruges, 1923), n. 533; Creusen, "Fondation de Maisons Religieuses,"—*Revue des Communautés Religieuses*, XI (1935), 99. (Hereafter this periodical is cited *RCR*.)

[14] "De Persona Morali,"—*Periodica*, X (1922), (34)-(35).

[15] Cf. cans. 1489 sqq.

[16] Can. 102, § 2.

[17] Can. 102, § 1.

[18] Larraona, "Commentarium Codicis,"—*CpR*, III (1922), 48. The dispersal of religious communities because of the disasters of war and civil perse-

Stability does not mean, however, that the religious community must own the building in which it resides, or that it must always remain in exactly the same place. These points will be discussed at greater length in another part of this work,[19] but for the purpose of clarity, it may be briefly mentioned at this point that a religious house can be juridically established in a rented building and that, under certain circumstances, it can be moved from place to place without losing its legal status or identity.

The final point one must note in analyzing the definition of a religious house is that it must be legitimately erected in order to enjoy the status of a true canonical house. This means that it must be erected with the authorization of competent ecclesiastical authority and be accepted by the religious superior of the institute in accordance with the norms of the constitutions. It is this act of canonical erection of a religious house which forms the subject matter of this work. Its concept is to be treated at length in the pages which follow.

Article 2. Kinds of Religious Houses

Canon 488, 5°, refers to only two species of religious houses: a regular house and a formal house. The canon defines a regular house as the house of a religious order. Hence the religious houses of all orders, whether the members be monks or nuns, clerks or canons regular, are designated by this term.[20] The Code has no specific term to indicate the religious house of a congregation. In referring to these houses it uses such expressions as, the *house of a religious congregation, the religious houses belonging to a congregation,* etc.[21] At other times it designates them by terms indicative of their purpose or character, as for instance, *novitiate, house of studies, college* and *hospice.*[22] Various other titles and designations

cution presents a special problem in this regard and is treated in Chapter X of this work.

[19] Cf. Chapter X.

[20] In various other canons, the Code also uses the term *monastery.* The term is synonymous with *regular house.* Cf., e. g., cans. 506; 512; 533; 535.

[21] Cf. cans. 498; 512, § 1, 2°; 604, §§ 1-2.

[22] Cf. cans. 554; 556; 587; 497, § 3.

for religious houses, such as, *convent*, *priory*, *cell*, etc., are found in the particular law of many institutes. These terms are correctly used within the limits of and with due conformity to the constitutions of the institute.

The second kind of religious house to which canon 488, 5°, refers is a *formal house.* This is defined as a house in which reside six professed religious, at least four of whom are priests, when there is question of a clerical institute.[23] It does not matter whether the vows of the six professed religious are perpetual or temporary, and, in the case of lay religious, the Code does not demand that the majority of the professed religious belong to the class of those capable of governing the community. Three professed choir sisters, for example, and three lay sisters, who are likewise professed, will constitute a formal house.[24]

The word *degunt,* which the Code uses in its definition of a formal house, must be taken in the sense of habitual residence. In other words, the religious who are staying in the house must be assigned there by the proper superior.[25] However, accidental absences for purpose of study, for performing acts of the sacred ministry, etc., do not affect the formal character of the house, unless there is fraud present, or unless the assignment is merely theoretical.[26] On the other hand, it cannot be argued on the basis of the principle stated in canon 102, § 2,[27] that a formal house remains such when it ceases to have the required number of members through the death or transfer of some of them. The text of the canon clearly implies that six religious must actually live in the house.

In the particular law of various institutes there may be other kinds or divisions of religious houses touching upon this distinction which the Code makes between formal and non-formal houses. Thus,

[23] Can. 488, 5° . . . domus formata est domus religiosa in qua sex saltem religiosi professi degunt, quorum, si agatur de religione clericali, quatuor sint sacerdotes.

[24] Creusen, *Religious Men and Women in the Code,* English translation by Garesché (3. English edition by Ellis, Milwaukee: Bruce, 1940), n. 11.

[25] Larraona, "Commentarium Codicis,"—*CpR,* III (1922), 52.

[26] Larraona, *loc. cit.*

[27] Can. 102, § 2: Si vel unum ex personae moralis collegialis membris supersit, ius omnium in illud recidit.

the constitutions may demand that a house have a certain number of members before it can send a delegate to the Chapter or exercise rights of a similar nature. The Code does not legislate for these kinds or divisions of houses, and the prescripts of the constitutions retain their force as regards the effects of particular law.

A third kind of religious house, which the Code does not define, but nevertheless implicitly recognizes in canon 497, § 3, is the *filial house.* The Holy See has expressly adopted this expression in a response of the Sacred Congregation of Religious.[28] One must be careful, however, to determine the sense in which the term *filial house* is used, for it has various connotations both in the constitutions of religious institutes and in the common language of the law. Thus, it is often applied in a general way to all religious houses which stem from the same mother house; or it may designate houses which have been established by religious who came originally from a great and important house of the same order or congregation. In this latter sense one speaks of the filial houses of Cluny, Beuron and Hotel Dieu. However, in neither of these two instances is the term *filial house* used in its strict and more proper sense. A strictly filial house, according to the concept which the Code recognizes in canon 497, § 3, and to the description given by the response of the Sacred Congregation, is an absolutely dependent house. It is not juridically distinct from the principal house to which it is attached, and its community is directly subject to the superior of this principal house as its immediate and proper superior. Hence a strictly filial house has no legal existence or moral personality apart from the independent religious house to which it is attached.[29]

A typical example of the strictly filial house is presented by the small communities of sisters who are sent by their superiors to direct a school which is attached to a principal house of the congregation. One of the sisters is usually placed in charge of the filial house, but she is only a delegate of the major or general superioress, and has only as much power as that superioress gives her.[30]

[28] S. C. de Relig., resp., 1 febr. 1924—*AAS,* XVI (1924), 95.

[29] Cf. Creusen, "Fondation de Maisons Religieuses,"—*RCR,* XI (1935) 65-66.

[30] Creusen, *loc. cit.* The sister in charge derives her power entirely from

In practice it is not always easy to determine whether a particular house is strictly filial, or whether it constitutes a true religious house, subject to all the formalities of canonical erection. The mere fact that a house is called a hospice, a quasi-residence, or a minor or secondary house, does not necessarily make it strictly filial, since these titles do not have a univocal meaning. Maroto (1875-1937) enumerates a number of conditions or circumstances which serve to indicate the character of strict filiality.[31] The most important of these conditions are:

1. The house does not constitute a true and distinct religious community, but is rather part of another house to which it is attached.

2. The religious in charge is only a simple delegate, revocable at will, of the superior, properly so-called, who resides in the principal house and governs the whole community.[32]

3. The house does not possess its own temporal goods.[33]

4. The religious exercise their capitular rights in the Chapter of the principal house.

The distinction between a true religious house and a strictly filial residence is important inasmuch as several canons of the Code, relative to religious houses, do not apply to filial houses.[34] Canon 497, § 3, in particular, makes it clear that permission of the Holy See is not necessary, even though an exempt institute is concerned, for the erection of houses which are strictly filial. A special permis-

personal commission (*ex commissione a persona*) and not from an office (*ex munere*).

[31] "Annotationes,"—*CpR,* V (1924), 122 sqq.

[32] Delegation by a local superior is found practically only in monasteries constituted under an abbot, or in independent houses of women religious in which the superioress is at the same time local and major superior. It would appear, however, that in institutes with centralized government a house may be strictly filial, even if the religious in charge is named by a major superior, as the provincial, rather than by a local superior, as long as the power given to this religious is entirely delegated. Cf. Vermeersch, "Annotationes,"—*Periodica,* XIII (1924), 55.

[33] This condition is not conclusive in itself, since in some institutes all goods belong to the institute itself or to one moral subject, as the general procurator.

[34] Creusen, "Fondation de Maisons Religieuses,"—*RCR,* XI (1935), 66.

sion of the local ordinary is required, but it also suffices for the opening or construction of these houses, whether they be exempt or non-exempt.

Vermeersch [85] makes a practical remark concerning filial houses when he states that the superior or general council of a religious institute cannot arbitrarily declare a house filial. The foundation must conform to the description of a filial house as given in the previously-mentioned response of the Sacred Congregation [86] and to the concept provided for in canon 497, § 3, of the Code. In other words, it must be a house which does not constitute a distinct community or possess its proper temporal goods, and which is governed by a simple delegate of a major superior, or of the superior of a principal house.

It may also be added, by way of practical comment, that the relations which filiality involves should actually be possible of attainment before one of these houses is established. Hence, if the community of a proposed house will be unable to recur easily and frequently to a true superior, its establishment as a filial house will be more apparent than real. Creusen [87] remarks in this respect that, if a rather large group of religious is sent to direct a hospital or similar institution, the maintenance of religious discipline and the right administration of the community will demand a certain measure of freedom of action and independent authority. He concludes, therefore, that unless there is another principal house in the same city, or at least very near by, to which this group can conveniently be attached, an institute can scarcely establish such a house as a strictly filial foundation.

Article 3. Canonical Erection

A. Meaning and Nature

Canonical erection, in the strict sense, is the concession of moral personality, that is, an act of competent ecclesiastical authority or a prescript of law by which an association or an institute is acknowl-

[85] "De Domibus Filialibus,"—*Periodica*, XVII (1928), 89*.

[86] Cf. page 30.

[87] "Fondation de Maisons Religieuses,"—*RCR*, XI (1935), 69.

edged as a moral person in the Church.[38] The canonical erection of a religious house, in particular, is the act of establishing a moral person pertaining to the religious state in a place where the community has a permanent residence. The act does not necessarily include the erection of a building or of a material edifice, for a religious house can be canonically erected in an existing building, purchased or rented by the institute.[39] It is necessary, however, to have a place of residence which is separated from the secular dwellings. This is required in order that the norms of the common law concerning the observance of the cloister may be fulfilled.[40] This condition is ordinarily satisfied as long as a separate section or floor of a building, such as a hospital, school or other institution, is set aside for the exclusive use of the religious community.

Several authorities concur in the canonical erection of a religious house. These are the internal authority of the religious institute, the local ordinary and, in some cases, the Holy See. The first act is ordinarily that of the competent superior of the institute and consists in a decision to establish a new house. The Code does not determine which superior is competent to make this decision. The constitutions of the institute will consequently provide the norm to be observed. In the case of congregations of simple vows, the *Normae* of 1901 require that the superior, before proceeding to establish a new religious house, obtain the consent of the council by means of a decisive vote.[41]

The decision of the competent religious superiors will have no effect until the necessary authorization of the local ordinary or, if the case demands, of the Holy See has been obtained. Although the authoritative decision of the religious superiors is the efficient cause which gives existence to a new religious house, the authorization of legitimate ecclesiastical authority is a necessary condition which must be fulfilled before this decision can have any juridical effect.[42] However, there is nothing to prevent the religious supe-

[38] Cf. can. 100, § 1; Larraona, "Commentarium Codicis,"—*CpR,* V (1924), 418.

[39] Coronata, *Institutiones,* n. 504.

[40] Cf. cans. 597-607.

[41] *Normae* of 1901, arts. 305, 271-272.

[42] Creusen, "Fondations de Maisons Religieuses,"—*RCR,* XI (1935), 103.

riors from gathering information concerning the advisability of the new foundation, inspecting the site, and even making a decision in the matter, before presenting a formal petition for approbation to the competent ecclesiastical authority. In fact, ordinary prudence will dictate such a procedure. The decision of the religious superiors will of course be conditioned on the granting of the necessary authorization by the local ordinary or the Holy See.

Any legitimately established religious institute can erect religious houses. The Code expressly acknowledges this right in canon 495, § 1, for institutes of diocesan right, and, in canon 497, § 1, it implicitly recognizes the same right for all other institutes.[43] Canonists disagree as to whether a formal decree of canonical erection must be issued by the superiors of the religious institute. Some authors hold that the mere fact of recognizing the house as part of the institute is sufficient, while others assert that a formal decree of erection is necessary. The latter opinion is upheld by Coronata [44] and Vromant.[45]

Coronata bases his argument on canon 100, § 1, and on a decree of the Sacred Congregation of Religious, [46] which declared that a formal decree of erection is necessary for the establishment of any diocesan institute or pious association. The argument, however, is not convincing. Canon 100, § 1, explicitly states that moral personality may arise not only as the result of a formal decree of competent authority, but also in consequence of the prescript of the law itself. The decree of the Sacred Congregation to which Coronata refers does not seem to form the basis of a valid argument of analogy. This decree relates to diocesan institutes and pious societies, which by their very nature can be established only by an authority which is external to the institute or society.[47]

In the case of erecting religious houses, however, the internal authority of the institute itself is capable of making the foundation.[48] The authorization of the local ordinary or of the Holy See is a nec-

[43] Schaefer, *De Religiosis*, n. 80, p. 126.

[44] *Institutiones*, n. 522.

[45] *De Bonis Ecclesiae Temporalibus* (Louvain: Desbarax, 1927), n. 19.

[46] 30 nov. 1922—*AAS*, XIV (1922), 644.

[47] Cf. cans. 491; 685.

[48] Can. 495, § 1.

essary condition for the validity of the foundation, but once this authorization has been given, the erection of the religious house is made by the competent religious superior, who, at least in fact, acknowledges the foundation as a religious house of his institute. Nowhere does the Code state that this acknowledgement must be made by means of a formal decree. Furthermore, the superiors of non-exempt institutes have no jurisdiction in the external forum. Consequently, even though they might issue a formal decree, they could not thereby concede moral personality to the new foundation. It must be concluded, therefore, that a decree of the religious superior is not necessary for the act of the canonical erection of a religious house. The law itself is the source of the legal personality which the new foundation enjoys. In other words, once the conditions prescribed by the canons are fulfilled, the religious house becomes a moral person by the prescript of the law itself.[49]

It is scarcely necessary to add, however, that prudence and good business methods will demand that the decision of the religious superiors to erect a new house and the acceptance of this house as a part of the institute be made in writing, and that a record be kept in the archives of the institute. This is a necessary precaution in order to prove in the external forum that the religious house has a true canonical status.[50]

The nature and necessity of the other acts of competent authority which concur in the canonical erection of a religious house, and to which reference was made at the beginning of this Article, will be treated at length in Chapter VII under the heading of requisite authorization.

B. Necessity

The norms prescribed by the canons pertinent to the erection of religious houses must be understood as applying only to houses in which the religious reside *as religious*. Hence villas, farmhouses and similar edifices, used for purely secular purposes, are not subject in the act of canonical erection to the formalities prescribed by canons

[49] Can. 100, § 1. Cf. Schaefer, *De Religiosis*, n. 80, p. 126; Larraona, "Commentarium Codicis,"—*CpR*, V (1924), 418; Creusen, "Fondation de Maisons Religieuses,"—*RCR*, XI (1935), 122.

[50] Schaefer, *De Religiosis*, n. 80, p. 126.

495-497. Moreover, as is pointed out in another part of this work, filial or dependent religious houses do not require the observance of the full solemnities of canonical erection.[51]

According to the norm of canon 497, § 3, the opening or erection of strictly filial houses, which are separated from a principal religious house, requires only a special written permission of the local ordinary. With due regard for this special and exceptional prescript laid down in canon 497, § 3, it may consequently be stated that, whenever the canons mention the erection, conversion or alteration of a religious house, one is to understand these prescriptions as referring only to a true religious house, that is, to a place in which a true and independent community has a fixed residence and carries out the proper works of the institute under the direction of its proper superior.[52]

The effects of any failure to observe the norms of canonical erection in the establishment of an independent religious house are far-reaching. The religious will be considered as living illegally in the house, and hence can claim none of the rights and privileges deriving from the fact of habitation in a religious house; they are unlawfully outside the cloister, and therefore subject to the prescriptions of canon 616.[53] Moreover, if the house in question is a novitiate house, the time passed there cannot count as the canonical year.[54] Finally, the rights which the law attributes to a canonically erected religious house as a moral person are forfeited.[55]

C. Effects

It has been already noted that the first and primary effect of the canonical erection is that it gives legal existence to the religious

[51] Cf. *infra,* pp. 96 sqq.

[52] Cf. Beste, *Introductio in Codicem* (St. John's Abbey: Collegeville, Minn., 1938), p. 321; Maroto, "Annotationes,"—*CpR,* V (1924), 126; cf. also *supra,* pp. 25 sqq.

[53] Can. 616, § 1: Regulares extra domum illegitime degentes, etiam sub praetextu accedendi ad Superiores, exemptionis privilegio non gaudent.

§ 2: Si extra domum delictum commiserint nec a proprio Superiore praemonito puniantur, a loci Ordinario puniri possunt. . . .

[54] Can. 555, § 1.

[55] Cf. division C. of this Article, below; cf. also, Fanfani, *De Iure Religiosorum* (ed. altera, Romae, 1925), n. 21.

house as a moral person.[56] The moral personality which an independent religious house enjoys before the law is a *collegiate* moral personality in so far as the community or religious family is concerned; it is a non-collegiate moral personality inasmuch as the religious house, taken in a material sense for the buildings and the temporal goods, which in accordance with the constitutions may be owned by the community, also obtains recognition before the law.[57]

From this status of the religious house as a moral person other rights also derive:

1. The religious house is held equal to a minor person by the law, and thus enjoys the rights and privileges of a person who is still in his minority.[58]

2. The foundation becomes by its nature perpetual. It can not be legally brought to extinction except through an act of suppression effected by the legitimate ecclesiastical authority, or through failure of members for a period of one hundred years.[59]

3. The religious house becomes legally capable of acquiring and owning temporal goods, unless this capacity is restricted or excluded by the constitutions.[60]

4. The house enjoys the local privileges of the institute to which it belongs.[61]

5. From the moment of its legitimate establishment the house begins to take its place of precedence with respect to other religious houses in the same locality.[62]

[56] Cf. page 33.

[57] Cf. cans. 99; 531; 532. Cf. also Schaefer, *De Religiosis,* n. 80, p. 128; n. 70, p. 106. It must be understood, however, that the religious house is not a non-collegiate moral person independently of the collegiate moral person, which is the religious community. An edifice is a religious house *because* it is the residence of a religious community. Cf. Creusen, "Fondation de Maisons Religieuses,"—*RCR,* XI (1935), 65.

[58] Cf. cans. 100, § 3; 1511, § 2; 1655, § 2; 1737.

[59] Can. 102, § 1.

[60] Can. 531.

[61] Cf. cans. 63 sqq.; 613.

[62] Can. 106, 5°. The rights consequent to the act which authorized the erection of a religious house may also be considered as effects of the canonical erection. These effects are treated in detail in Chapter VIII.

D. Canonical Erection and the Civil Law

The Catholic Church is by its very nature and by divine ordination a perfect society[63] and is therefore endowed with the native right of administering her own internal affairs, independently of any civil government. Since the erection of religious houses is in itself a purely ecclesiastical act, it follows that the Church alone has the right to impose norms pertinent to their establishment. However, the fact that the acquisition and ownership of property is ordinarily involved in the establishment of a religious house often brings this matter into conflict with the statutes of civil governments. In order to prevent greater evils, the Church has agreed, in many instances, to observe the formalities required by civil law. In making this concession, however, the Church does not renounce any of her native rights as a perfect society, but, for reasons of prudence, simply relinquishes their exercise.

The Holy See has drawn up concordats with the governments of many nations as a means of both asserting and defending her rights in her relationships with these governments. Canon 3 declares that the Code does not in any way affect the terms of concordats contracted previous to the time of its adoption. Concordats, entered into since the promulgation of the Code, must be considered as particular law, binding those persons, things and actions which are embraced by their terms. Hence, if the Church agrees by concordat to observe certain formalities of civil law in the erection of religious houses, these formalities must be observed.[64]

In the United States, civil law, although failing to recognize com-

[63] Cf. Goodwine, *The Right of the Church to Acquire Temporal Goods*, The Catholic University of America Canon Law Studies, n. 131 (Washington, D. C.: The Catholic University of America Press, 1941), pp. 6 sqq.

The Vatican Council had prepared a statement defining the Church's status as a perfect society, but due to the suspension of the Council this *schema* never became law; cf. Goodwine, *op. cit.*, p. 94. The proposed canon read as follows: "Si quis dixerit Ecclesiam non esse societatem perfectam sed collegium; aut ita in civili societate seu in statu esse, ut saeculari dominationi subiciatur: anathema sit"—*Acta et Decreta Sacrorum Conciliorum Recentiorum, Collectio Lacensis* (7 vols., Friburgi Brisgoviae, 1870-1890), VII, 577.

[64] Wernz-Vidal, *Ius Canonicum ad Codicis Normam Exactum*, III, *De Religiosis* (Romae: Apud Aedes Universitatis Gregorianae, 1933), n. 78.

pletely the plenary claims of the Church as a juristic personality, has nevertheless by statute and by judicial decree, generally recognized the corporation sole, the diocesan or parish corporation and other religious aggregate entities and their basic rights to acquire and administer property.[65] Hence, American civil law will undoubtedly permit incorporation under secular law of a canonically erected religious house, so that it may have in secular law that legal status which it enjoys by the prescript of canon law.

[65] White, "Certain Aspects of the Legal Status of the Church in the United States,"—*The Jurist,* I (1941), 21; cf. Brown, *The Canonical Juristic Personality with Special Reference to Its Status in the United States of America,* The Catholic University of America Canon Law Studies, n. 39 (Washington, D. C.: The Catholic University of America, 1927), p. 131.

CHAPTER VI

PREREQUISITE CONDITIONS FOR THE ERECTION OF ALL RELIGIOUS HOUSES

Canon 496: Nulla religiosa domus erigatur, nisi iudicari prudenter possit vel ex reditibus propriis vel ex consuetis eleemosynis vel alio modo congruae sodalium habitationi et sustenationi provisum iri.

Article 1. The Code and Former Legislation

The conditions which must be fulfilled before permission can be granted for the erection of any religious house are laid down in canon 496. This canon states that no religious house shall be established unless, according to prudent judgment, the community will be able to support itself properly, either by fixed income or by the usual alms or by other means. All religious houses—formal and non-formal, exempt and non-exempt, houses of regulars and those of congregations—are included in this prescript.[1]

The present law is a mitigation of pre-Code legislation and, as is evident from the text of the canon, allows a greater measure of freedom to the prudent judgment of the competent authority. The more precise norms of the old law concerning the number of religious necessary to form a community and the obligation of the local ordinary to consult the superiors of other institutes are not repeated in the Code. These prescripts, therefore, do not retain their force in the present discipline.[2]

The former law required twelve religious to form the community of a true religious house.[3] The only prescript of the Code in this regard is that of canon 488, 5°, which requires six professed religious

[1] Residences which are not true religious houses, such as villas, hospices, farmhouses, etc., are not included; cf. *supra*, page 25.

[2] Can. 6, 6°.

[3] Cf. const. *"Cum alias,"* 27 aug. 1622—*Bull. Roman. Taur.*, XII, 719.

to constitute a formal house. The number of religious requisite but sufficient to constitute a non-formal house is not determined by the Code. However, the group must number at least three, in order to constitute a true community,[4] and, on the other hand, the norm of canon 496 demands that the community must not be so numerous that the revenues will be inadequate to support it properly. Battandier (1850-1921) declares that the Holy See is opposed to the establishment of independent houses with a community of less than four religious. In support of his assertion he cites annotations of the Sacred Congregation of Religious on the occasion of granting approval to the constitutions of several institutes of women religious.[5]

In the matter of consulting the superiors of nearby religious houses, Prümmer (1866-1931) holds that the conditions imposed by the papal constitutions still retain their force inasmuch as they are based upon the very nature of the act of canonical erection of a new religious house.[6] However, it appears more correct to say that natural equity will often demand that these norms be used as a criterion to safeguard the rights and needs of other communities which are located in the place where the new foundation is to be made. In practice, it will often be necessary for the local ordinary to consult the superiors of these other institutes in order to discharge the obligation imposed upon him by canon 496. If there be a number of these communities in the neighborhood, the local ordinary can scarcely form a prudent judgment concerning the possibility of adequate support for the new religious house, unless he investigates the needs of the houses already established in the vicinity.

The Code provides a remedy for the violation of the rights of communities already established in the place where it is proposed to erect a new religious house in the legal action of *Nuntiatio Novi Operis*. Hence, if the local ordinary authorizes the erection of a new house and the superiors of these already existing communities believe that their rights will be prejudiced, they may seek an injunction against the proposed foundation until the rights of both parties have been decided by judicial sentence.[7]

[4] Note, however, the view of Vermeersch as stated on page 27 of this work.

[5] *Guide Canonique pour les Instituts à Voeux Simples*, n. 513.

[6] *Manuale Iuris Canonici* (3. ed., Friburgi Brisgoviae, 1922), q. 181, p. 241.

[7] Can. 1676.

The extent to which the rights of a pastor must be respected, when a religious house is to be established in his territory, was disputed among pre-Code canonists.[8] The common opinion held that he had only the right to appeal a decision after the fact and that it was not necessary to consult him beforehand. The present law requires that the local ordinary shall consult the pastors whose interests are involved only when a church or public oratory is to be opened in connection with the religious house.[9]

Under the old law the so-called *privilegium cannarum* was granted by the Holy See to many religious orders. In virtue of this privilege these institutes had the right to forbid the erection of other houses within a distance which varied, according to the tenor of the indult, from one hundred and forty to three hundred paces. According to the norm of canon 4 this privilege, provided that it was still in use at the time of the adoption of the Code, still retains its force, since it is not expressly revoked by the canons.[10] It is the opinion of many canonists, however, that this privilege had passed out of use to such an extent before the promulgation of the Code that it is no longer of any practical moment.[11] Contrary privileges which were granted, permitting religious institutes to disregard the *privilegium cannarum*, and the fact that religious congregations were not strictly bound by it, rendered the privilege ineffective and caused it to fall into desuetude.[12] In practice, therefore, the *privilegium cannarum* can be invoked only in rare instances as a particular privilege by some order which has not lost it through lack of use when it is not in conflict with contrary privileges.

The Instruction of the Sacred Congregation of Religious, which forbade an institute to contract debts in order to erect a religious house, no longer binds.[13] Although this instruction may still be used

[8] Cf. *supra*, page 13.

[9] Can. 1162, § 3.

[10] Cf. cans. 4 and 613, § 1.

[11] Coronata, *Institutiones*, n. 523; Pejška, *Ius Canonicum Religiosorum*, p. 52; Larraona, "Commentarium Codicis,"—*CpR*, V (1924), 333, and note 233; Vermeersch-Creusen, *Epitome Iuris Canonici*, I (4. ed., Mechlinae, Romae, 1929), n. 563. (Hereafter this work is cited as *Epitome*.)

[12] Vermeersch-Creusen, *Epitome*, loc. cit.

[13] S. C. de Relig., instr., 30 iul. 1909—*AAS*, I (1909), 697.

as a directive norm in forming the prudent judgment required by canon 496, it is now only necessary, in strict law, to observe the canons which regulate the alienation of ecclesiastical goods and the contracting of debts.[14]

Article 2. Obligation of the Prudent Judgment

. . . nisi iudicari prudenter possit . . . congruae sodalium habitationi et sustentationi provisum iri.

The obligation to form a prudent judgment or estimate that the temporal support of the new religious house will be assured pertains to the licitness and not to the validity of the act of consent necessary to erect it.[15] Only those laws are to be considered invalidating which expressly or equivalently state that an act is null and void.[16] The text of canon 496 contains no clause which could be adduced as expressing invalidity for failure to observe its norms.

The Code does not specify the person or persons upon whom the obligation of forming a prudent judgment is incumbent. Fanfani asserts that it belongs to the bishop of the place.[17] He bases his opinion on the argument that this judgment was reserved to the bishop in pre-Code law.[18] Since the present legislation still requires the consent of the local ordinary for the erection of a religious house, Fanfani concludes that the obligation of making the prudent judgment, which must precede the act of consent, is also incumbent upon the local ordinary.

It is the more common opinion of canonists, however, that this obligation belongs by equal right to the local ordinary and the competent religious superior.[19] This opinion is more in conformity

[14] Cf. cans. 534; 1530-1533; 1538. Cf. also can. 549, which forbids the use of dowries to erect a religious house during the lifetime of the nuns who have brought them.

[15] Coronata, *Institutiones*, n. 523; Schaefer, *De Religiosis*, n. 83, p. 133.

[16] Can. 11.

[17] *De Iure Religiosorum*, n. 21.

[18] Cf. const. "*Quoniam*," 23 iul. 1603—*Fontes*, n. 190.

[19] Coronata, *Institutiones*, n. 523; Larraona, "Commentarium Codicis,"—*CpR*, V (1924), 332, and note 231; Farrell, *The Rights and Duties of the Local Ordinary Regarding Congregations of Women Religious of Pontifical Approval*,

with the very nature of the act of establishing a new religious house, which demands that both the local ordinary and the religious superior consider, from their respective viewpoints, the needs of the new foundation and estimate the possibility of meeting these needs. The local ordinary, in virtue of his position, is competent to judge the needs, opportunities and possibilities of the locality where the house is to be erected. The religious superior, on the other hand, is qualified to judge the needs of the religious community.[20] The burden of judgment, therefore, should not be thrown exclusively upon one party. However, the final decision to the effect that suitable provision is or is not assured will rest with the local ordinary, for he may not grant the requisite authorization to erect the house until he has this assurance.

Absolute and mathematical certitude of adequate provision for the new religious house is neither required nor possible. A prudent moral judgment is sufficient. In forming this prudent moral judgment, the following factors should be considered:

(a) The needs to be met and the opportunities afforded in the particular locality should be weighed. Neither the local ordinary nor the religious superior should desire to establish a house unless there is a definite need to be fulfilled and there exists an opportunity to supply that need in the place proposed as a site. The work of other religious and of the members of the secular clergy, who are established in the locality, should not be compromised nor should their means of support be diminished, without proportionate benefit. Thus, if it is the intention of the institute to open a school or hospital in connection with the proposed house, the existence of other schools and hospitals in the locality would ordinarily render the support of another community, dedicated to the same kind of work, rather precarious.[21] Rivalry and competition might easily imperil not only the existence

The Catholic University of America Canon Law Studies, n. 128 (Washington, D. C.: The Catholic University of America Press, 1941), 58. (Hereafter this work will be cited *The Local Ordinary and Women Religious of Pontifical Approval.*)

[20] Farrell, *op. cit.*, p. 59.

[21] Cf. Creusen, "Fondation de Maisons Religieuses,"—*RCR,* XI (1935), 102.

of the new community, but of already established houses as well.[22] The elementary principles of prudence, justice and charity demand that such circumstances be taken into consideration by both the local ordinary and the religious superiors.

(b) The amount of temporal aid that the new house will require must be estimated and a comparison made between this amount and the certain or potential possibilities of supplying it. On the one hand, there must be reckoned the expense of constructing and furnishing the house, the cost of equipment and materials which the religious will need to carry on their work, and the necessary provision for living expenses, such as food, clothing and adequate medical care. On the other hand, the sources of income upon which the community will have to depend must be estimated and balanced against the various needs which are to be met.[23]

The Code demands assurance of suitable (*congrua*) lodging and support for the religious community. This prescript allows a certain measure of flexibility, since it is necessarily relative to other factors, such as the rule of the institute, the degree to which the constitutions require the observance of poverty, and the place where the house is to be located. Very different standards of living will prevail in mission territory, for instance, or in a poor locality than in a prosperous city. Augustine attempts to set a criterion which may serve as a standard of what is suitable or congruous for all religious under ordinary circumstances. He states that the lodging of the community should be such that a man of modest aspirations, for example, of the middle class, would be content with it. The same may be said also of support. It is not luxuries which are to be sought in a religious house, but a modest living, gauged by the amount and kind of work performed by the religious, and the ordinary comforts to which a self-respecting human being is entitled.[24]

(c) The nature and purpose of the proposed religious house must be considered and adjudged in relation to the place where it is to be established. The rule of life of the institute, the kind of work to be

[22] Cf. Augustine, *Religious and Laymen*, p. 85.

[23] These sources of income are treated in detail in the Article immediately following.

[24] *Religious and Laymen*, p. 86.

undertaken in the house, and the circumstance of whether its members are men or women religious will be the important factors in this consideration. If the chief work of the community is to be that of teaching school, doing parish work or engaging in other active works of the ministry, then adequate income to provide for its needs may be practically assured. On the other hand, if it is a mendicant community, bound by the law of strict cloister, it cannot be prudently expected to obtain adequate support from alms alone, if the house is to be erected in a remote or very poor place. Provision for suitable support in this case must be assured from other sources, such as income from property or from the dowries of the members.[25]

The character of the proposed house will also enter into consideration. Houses of study, for instance, and houses of novitiate and postulancy are usually supported by the institute itself. Hence, if the house to be established is intended for one of these purposes, nothing more is required than assurance that the institute will be able to bear the added burden.[26]

Article 3. Means of Support

. . . ex reditibus propriis vel ex consuetis eleemosynis vel alio modo. . . .

The means of support which the Code enumerates are the proper revenues of the house, alms and other sources of income. By *proper revenues* is meant a regular and dependable income derived from property owned by the community or from the industry of its members. One may include under this heading, therefore, revenue from real estate, safely invested capital, stocks and bonds, and income from corporeal or incorporeal rights possessed by the community. Also, since they are usually dependable sources of revenue, it appears that one may include in this term income from dowries, tuition of students and salaries paid to members of the community for work done in schools, hospitals, parishes, etc.[27]

[25] Augustine, *Religious and Laymen,* p. 85.

[26] Larraona, "Commentarium Codicis,"—*CpR,* V (1924), 333.

[27] Augustine, *Religious and Laymen,* p. 83.

The term *usual alms* refers to those free-will offerings of the faithful which the religious house can normally expect to receive. In this respect the norms of canons 621-622, which govern the right of religious institutes to beg alms, must be taken into consideration. Only the strictly mendicant orders have the right by law to ask for alms. Other religious institutes are forbidden to beg, except on the following conditions: an institute of pontifical approval must obtain a special permission of the Holy See and the written permission of the ordinary of the place where its members wish to beg; a diocesan institute must obtain the written permission of the ordinary of the diocese in which their principal house is located as well as the consent of the ordinary of the place where they desire to collect alms.[28]

Geser [29] states that the term *usual alms* may be used only in reference to the mendicant orders, strictly so-called, since they alone have the legal right by common law to collect alms. However, this opinion seems to be an unwarranted restriction of the term *usual alms* as used by the Code. It is true that only the strictly mendicant religious have the right to beg alms from door to door (*ius quaestuandi*), but all religious institutes may accept alms. Therefore, the word "usual" appears to denote here "customary," "ordinary" or "regular," that is, the alms which the institute can normally count upon. Thus, if a religious community has special benefactors whose offerings can be depended on as a source of assured income, these offerings seem to be included in the term *usual* alms.

The Code adds a third means of support to the two traditional sources of revenue by saying: *vel alio modo.* This means of support is practically unlimited in its scope. In contradistinction to the traditional forms of income, however, it embraces those sources or modes of revenues which are more or less irregular and variable in character. In the case of many religious communities, income from such sources can prudently be assured and even approximately estimated. For instance, religious houses which are established in connection

[28] Cans. 621-622. It may also be noted here that local ordinaries, especially those of nearby dioceses, should not deny or recall this permission to beg alms, except for grave and urgent reasons, if the religious house can not get sufficient support from the alms collected in its own diocese. Cf. can. 621, § 2.

[29] *The Canon Law Governing Communities of Sisters* (St. Louis: Herder, 1938), n. 138.

with a hospital, a home for the orphans or the aged, or a similar charitable institution, often depend in great measure upon donations. These donations, in many cases, take the form of participation in the proceeds of a diocesan collection, or of contributions made by the state, municipality or diocese in return for service rendered by the religious in the hospital, orphanage, etc.[80]

Other means of support which may be included under this general classification are legacies, income from patents and copyrights and royalties on books.[81]

[80] Creusen, "Fondation de Maisons Religieuses,"—*RCR,* XI (1935), 101.

[81] Augustine, *Religious and Laymen,* p. 84.

CHAPTER VII

AUTHORIZATION NECESSARY TO ERECT A RELIGIOUS HOUSE

Canon 495, § 1: Congregatio religiosa iuris dioecesani in alia dioecesi domos constituere non potest, nisi consentiente utroque Ordinario, tum loci ubi est domus princeps, tum loci quo velit commigrare; Ordinarius autem loci unde excedit, consensum sine gravi causa ne deneget.

Canon 497, § 1: Ad erigendam domum religiosam exemptam, sive formatam sive non formatam, aut monasterium monialium, aut in locis Sacrae Congregationi de Prop. Fide subiectis quamlibet religiosam domum, requiritur beneplacitum Sedis Apostolicae et Ordinarii loci consensus in scriptis datus; secus satis est Ordinarii venia.

Article 1. Authorization in General

A. Meaning and Efficacy

The Code uses various terms in referring to the authorization of the competent superior which is necessary for the erection of a religious house. It mentions the *licentia, venia* and *consensus* of the local ordinary, and the *beneplacitum* of the Holy See. It is evident from the context of the legislation, however, that all of these terms are practically synonymous. Whether the Code mentions *permission, favor, consent* or *approbation* in these canons, the meaning is the same: an act of express consent on the part of the competent ecclesiastical superior is necessary for the erection of a religious house. This consent is an act of ecclesiastical jurisdiction and has the efficacy of a condition which must be fulfilled in order that a religious house may obtain legal status as such before the law.

Most canonists hold that the approbation required by law pertains to the validity of the act of canonical erection.[1] They state, without any qualification or distinction, that an omission of this requisite permission results in juridical nullity of the foundation.

Vromant, however, proposes a distinction between papal and episcopal approbation, holding the former to be necessary for validity, while considering the latter to pertain to the legal stability *(firmitas)* of the religious foundation, but not to its existence.[2]

In common with the rest of the authors, Vromant asserts that the omission of papal approval, when this is required by law, certainly nullifies the act of canonical erection. The basis of this opinion is an argument drawn from pre-Code doctrine and practice. Innocent X, in the Constitution "*Instaurandae,*" not only stated a canonical penalty for regulars who presumed to erect a religious house without requisite permission, but also decreed that foundations so made were by the law itself null and void.[3] Likewise, the letter of the Sacred Congregation of the Propagation of the Faith, previously mentioned, stated that a canonical ratification should be asked from the Holy See to sanate foundations which had been made without the approval of the Sacred Congregation.[4] Thus it implicitly declared that religious houses erected in mission territory were invalidly established, if the permission of the Sacred Congregation had been omitted.

The same law must be said to prevail now after the Code, in accordance with the principles enunciated in canon 6, 3° and 4°, and in canon 20.[5] This conclusion is further supported by a response

[1] Cf. Schaefer, *De Religiosis,* n. 80, p. 128; Fanfani, *De Iure Religiosorum,* n. 21; Vermeersch-Creusen, *Epitome,* I, n. 560; Farrell, *The Local Ordinary and Women Religious of Pontifical Approval,* 62; Larraona, "Commentarium Codicis,"—*CpR,* V (1924), 424.

[2] "De Licentiis Requisitis ad Erigendam Domum Religiosam,"—*Jus Pontificium,* VIII (1928), 213. This opinion is also supported by Berutti (*Institutiones Iuris Canonici,* III [Taurini, 1936], 36-37).

[3] Const. "*Instaurandae,*" 15 oct. 1652, § 5—*Fontes,* n. 233.

[4] S. C. Prop. Fide, litt. encycl., 7 dec. 1901—*ASS,* XXXIV (1901-1902), 639; *Fontes,* n. 4938; *Coll. S. C. P. F.,* n. 2126.

[5] Canon 6, 3°: Canones qui ex parte tantum cum veteri iure congruunt, qua congruunt, ex iure antiquo aestimandi sunt . . . ;

4°: In dubio num aliquod canonum praescriptum cum veteri iure discrepet, a veteri iure non est recedendum.

of the Sacred Congregation of Religious to a doubt proposed by various bishops. The question was asked: Are nuns whose vows are simple in virtue of a prescript of the Holy See permitted to erect a monastery, without papal approbation, in places where this prescript is not in force? The Sacred Congregation replied in the negative and added that the Holy See was to be asked for a sanation for houses which had been erected without this approbation.[6]

The omission of the consent of the local ordinary, according to Vromant,[7] seems to render the act of canonical erection only incompletely invalid, that is, relatively null or rescissible. Modern canonists commonly agree that the granting of requisite consent by the local ordinary *after the fact* is sufficient to validate a foundation.[8] This opinion is based on pre-Code doctrine as taught by Fagnanus [9] and confirmed by Pius IX (1846-1878) in a letter to Archbishop Darboy of Paris.[10]

Complete invalidity requires the positing of a new act, endowed with all the conditions required by law, or a sanation in order to render it valid. However, the sanation of an act which is invalid by prescript of universal law is reserved exclusively to the Roman Pontiff.[11] Therefore, if the ratification of the local ordinary, given after the fact of foundation, is sufficient to produce the effects required by law, it follows that his permission is not necessary to the extent that

Canon 20: Si certa de re desit expressum praescriptum legis sive generalis sive particularis, norma sumenda est . . . a stylo et praxi Curiae Romanae a communi constantique sententia doctorum.

[6] S. C. de Relig., resp., 11 oct. 1922, ad II—*AAS,* XIV (1922), 555.

[7] *Loc. cit.*

[8] Cf. Coronata, *Institutiones,* n. 523, p. 638, note 8; Vermeersch-Creusen, *Epitome,* I, n. 560; Bondini, *De Privilegio Exemptionis seu de Regularium Immunitate ab Ordinariorum Locorum Iurisdictione prout in Novo Iuris Canonici Codice Sancitur* (Romae, 1919), pp. 43-44.

[9] *Commentarium in Librum Decretalium,* lib. III, *de institutionibus,* cap. *non amplius,* n. 58.

[10] ". . . Nam te minime latet hunc esse proprium, naturalem et iuridicum omnis ratihabitionis . . . effectum, sanandi scilicet defectum illius actus qui praecedere debuisset. . . ."—*ASS,* XI (1878), 217. The letter is dated Oct. 26, 1865.

[11] Cf. S. C. C., *Albinganen. et aliarum,* 17 maii 1919—*AAS,* XI (1919), 386; cf. also cans. 586, § 1, and 1141.

the act of erecting a religious house will be completely invalid without this consent. If it were otherwise, that is, if the act of canonical erection were completely invalid without the ordinary's consent, his mere ratification of the foundation would not suffice; either he would have to repeat the act, complete with all its formalities, or he would have to seek a sanation from the Holy See.[12]

On the other hand, the fact that ratification of the local ordinary is necessary, whenever a house has been erected without his permission, makes it evident that the omission of his consent results in a foundation which is at least rescissible. Hence, it may be concluded that a local ordinary who, for a just reason, does not wish to ratify the erection of a house made without his consent, may recur to the proper Congregation of the Holy See—the Sacred Congregation of Religious or the Sacred Congregation of the Propagation of the Faith—and petition that the foundation be declared null by that body.[13]

This opinion as proposed by Vromant appears to be based on arguments which are juridically sound. However, the distinction between papal and episcopal authorization, with regard to their respective effect upon the validity of a new religious house, seems to be applicable only to the case in which the permission of both of these authorities is required by law.[14] In other words, the omission of the local ordinary's consent in a case which requires *only* his own authorization for the validity of the canonical erection seems to result in a foundation which is not merely rescissible, but actually invalid.

The opinion which holds that a ratification by the local ordinary is sufficient for the validity is based solely on the letter of Pope Pius IX and his confirmation of the teaching of Fagnanus in this regard. Now, it is evident from the context of the Pontiff's letter that he was instructing the Archbishop concerning the juridical status of some religious houses which had received papal approbation, but

[12] Vromant, "De Licentiis Requisitis ad Erigendam Domum Religiosam,"—*Jus Pontificium,* VIII (1928), 215.

[13] Vromant, *loc. cit.*

[14] Although Vromant is not explicit in the matter, he nevertheless seems implicitly to restrict his interpretation to this case, that is, when the permission of both the Holy See and the local ordinary is required.

which, for some reason, had never obtained episcopal approbation. The Pope cited the doctrine of Fagnanus in the matter and informed the Archbishop that when a foundation had received the approval of the Apostolic See, it was sufficient for validity that the local ordinary simply ratify the act. It is clear, therefore, that this letter of Pius IX did not refer to religious houses which had been erected without *any* permission.

Therefore, when the law requires only the permission of the local ordinary for the canonical establishment of a religious house, it seems certain that the *previous* consent of the local ordinary is necessary for validity. A contrary opinion would place one in conflict with the practically unanimous opinion of all canonists, and would lead to the seemingly untenable conclusion that a religious house which is erected without any permission whatsoever connotes only a rescissible foundation and not an invalid one. The entire history of the legislation on religious houses reveals that such a conclusion is juridically unsound.

Another point which canonists discuss in connection with the question of valid authorization concerns the formality with which this consent must be given. The point at issue may be summarized in two related questions to be discussed concurrently: Must the permission of the local ordinary be always granted in writing? Does the failure to observe this formality invalidate the act of the canonical erection?[15]

Canon 497, § 1, expressly states that the consent of the local ordinary must be given in writing for the erection of a religious house which requires papal approbation as well as his own permission. A doubt arises, however, when the law demands only the ordinary's consent. Canon 495, § 1, does not specify a written consent of the ordinaries for the erection of houses of diocesan right, and the final clause of canon 497, § 1, states only: *secus satis est Ordinarii venia,* that is, for religious houses not mentioned in the first clause of the canon the approbation of the ordinary is sufficient.

[15] As stated in the discussion immediately preceding, it cannot be proved that the failure to obtain even the oral consent of the local ordinary effects anything more than a relative nullity when the previous permission of the Holy See has been obtained. Hence the omission of the formality of writing can at most render the foundation rescissible in this particular case.

Many canonists contend that even in these cases, where it is not expressly demanded, the consent of the local ordinary must nevertheless be given in writing.[16] Larraona discusses the question at length [17] and bases his opinion for the necessity of a written permission on three main arguments:

1. The context of canon 497, § 1, clearly indicates that a written permission of the local ordinary is necessary for *all* religious houses. The consent of the local ordinary which is required for houses which also need papal approbation is identical with the act of consent which the local ordinary must give when only his own permission is prescribed by law. Hence, if this permission must be given in writing in one case, as the law expressly states, it must also be given in writing for the other case as well.

2. Canon 497, § 3, requires a special written permission of the local ordinary for the opening or construction of a school, hospice or similar edifice, separated from the religious house. Edifices of this kind depend upon and pertain to an established religious house. They have no independent juridical existence. Therefore, if a written permission is necessary to open or construct one of these dependent edifices, the same formality must be observed for the erection of the independent religious house to which they are attached.

3. The Code demands a written consent of the local ordinary for the erection of lay associations,[18] for the aggregation of associations to a confraternity,[19] and for the erection of a church or public oratory.[20] On the basis of analogy, therefore, it would seem that written permission is equally necessary for the erection of a religious house, which is a matter of ecclesiastical discipline of at least equal importance.

Larraona concludes from these arguments that a written consent of the local ordinary is necessary, even when the text of the Code does not expressly demand this formality. Furthermore, he adds

[16] Larraona, "Commentarium Codicis,"—*CpR,* I (1920), 112-114; Pejška, *Ius Canonicum Religiosorum,* p. 52; Fanfani, *De Iure Religiosorum,* n. 21; Oesterle, *Praelectiones Iuris Canonici,* I (Romae, 1931), 246.

[17] Larraona, *loc. cit.*

[18] Can. 686, § 3.

[19] Can. 723, 2°.

[20] Cans. 1162, § 1, and 1191, § 1.

that it is necessary for the validity of the act of the canonical erection, since the permission of the local ordinary pertains to the substantial form of the act in the same manner as does the papal approbation. The style and practice of the Roman Curia, according to Larraona, have held that the written consent of the Holy See pertains to the validity of the act of the canonical erection of a religious house, and there is no reason for the written permission of the local ordinary to be any less substantial to the act, since it is equally required.[21]

The writer agrees with Larraona's contention that the permission of the local ordinary *ought* to be given in writing, even when the canons do not expressly demand this solemnity. But the conclusion that a failure to observe this formality results in the nullity of the act of the canonical erection is not convincing. Larraona's statement that the doctrine and practice of the Roman Curia have held the written consent of the Holy See to be necessary for the validity of the act is not supported, for, although it is true that the practice of the Curia is always to grant the requisite permission in writing, it does not follow from this that, if it is granted only orally, the consent would be invalid. Certainly this cannot be proved from the Code which does not impose norms upon the Holy See.

The formality of a written consent seems rather to be an accidental solemnity which the Code prescribes for the purpose of meeting the possible eventual need of establishing by means of an authentic document the certain and legitimate erection of a religious house. In support of this statement one may adduce the jurisprudence of the old law, which held that the formality of a written consent did not pertain to the substance of the act of the canonical erection of a religious house.[22] Custom brought it about that the permission of the local ordinary was usually given in writing in order to provide an expeditious means of proving the canonical status of a religious house.[23] The Code appears to have made this solemnity a

[21] "Commentarium Codicis,"—*CpR,* V (1924), 114.

[22] Schmalzgrueber, *Ius Ecclesiasticum Universum,* lib. III, tit. 7, n. 39; Piatus Montensis, *Praelectiones Iuris Regularis* (3. ed., 2 vols., Tornaci, 1906), II, 264.

[23] Schmalzgrueber, *loc. cit.*

directive precept for the same reason: a written consent affords an indisputable proof in the external forum that a religious house has been canonically erected.

One may conclude, therefore, that the local ordinary ought always to grant his permission for the erection of a religious house in written form, not however for the validity of the act, but rather for the purpose of providing a suitable means of proof whereby the accomplished fact of the canonical erection can be readily substantiated before the law. The authority of canonists who hold that a written permission of the local ordinary is not necessary for the validity of the act of the canonical erection is sufficiently great to render not only probable, but practically certain, the validity of an oral consent.[24]

B. The Competent Local Ordinary

The local ordinary whose consent is required by the canons on the erection of religious houses may be the bishop of a diocese, a prefect or vicar apostolic, or a prelate or abbot *nullius*. Canonists disagree as to whether or not the vicar general and the vicar capitular of a diocese are included within the scope of the term *local ordinary* as used in these canons.

In the old law the question was equally controverted, but the common opinion held that the vicar general needed a special mandate in order to authorize the erection of a religious house. The establishment of new religious houses was considered to be a matter of serious importance to a diocese, and consequently the power to permit their erection was regarded as being excluded from the general concession of faculties granted by law to the vicar general.[25]

Many post-Code canonists argue that the former discipline with regard to the vicar general remains unchanged on the basis of the

[24] Coronata, *Institutiones*, n. 523; Schaefer, *De Religiosis*, n. 80, p. 128; Berutti, *Institutiones Iuris Canonici*, III, 37; Raus, *Institutiones Canonicae iuxta Novum Codicem Iuris* (2. ed., Parisiis; Vitte, 1931), n. 177; De Meester, *Juris Canonici et Juris Canonico-Civilis Compendium*, I (Bruges, 1921), 391, note 4. (Hereafter this work is cited *Compendium*.)

[25] Piatus Montensis, *Praelectiones Iuris Regularis*, II, 260; Bouix, *De Iure Regularium*, tom. I, pars II, sect. 2, cap. 2, n. 2.

principle enunciated in canon 6, 2°.[26] Hence they assert that the vicar general cannot authorize the erection of a religious house without a special mandate.

Goyeneche argues the case for the negative opinion at length, basing his stand upon the following arguments:

1. The vicar general cannot give permission to erect a church without a special mandate.[27] But for a clerical institute the permission to erect a religious house carries with it the right to have a church or public oratory attached to the house. Therefore, with respect to clerical institutes at least, the vicar general is not competent to authorize the erection of a religious house.

2. The vicar general is forbidden to perform other legal actions which are less important than the authorization of a religious house. He cannot permit, for instance, the erection of pious associations; [28] he cannot consecrate places,[29] give dimissorials [30] or authenticate relics.[31] *A fortiori*, therefore, he cannot permit the establishment of a religious house which is a more serious matter of diocesan discipline.

3. In the old law the common opinion held that the vicar general needed a special mandate to grant the authorization in question. Since the former discipline remains unchanged, it is necessary to interpret the law now as formerly.[32]

Berutti,[33] Coronata [34] and Campagna,[35] the latter with certain

[26] Canones qui ius vetus ex integro referunt, ex veteris iuris auctoritate, atque ideo ex receptis apud probatos auctores interpretationibus, sunt aestimandi.

In favor of this opinion are Larraona ("Commentarium Codicis,"—*CpR*, V [1924], 424), Schaefer (*De Religiosis*, n. 88, p. 141) and Goyeneche ("Consultationes,"—*CpR*, I [1920], 114 sqq.).

[27] Can. 1162, § 1.

[28] Can. 684.

[29] Can. 1155.

[30] Can. 988.

[31] Can. 1283.

[32] Goyeneche, "Consultationes,"—*CpR*, I (1920), 115.

[33] *Institutiones Iuris Canonici*, III, 43.

[34] *Institutiones*, n. 523.

[35] *Il Vicario Generale del Vescovo*, The Catholic University of America Canon Law Studies, n. 66 (Washington, D. C.: The Catholic University of America, 1931), p. 141.

reservations, assert that the vicar general is competent to authorize the erection of a religious house in virtue of his ordinary power.

In support of this view, the arguments of Goyeneche for the negative opinion may be discussed in turn and an attempt made to refute them. Goyeneche's first argument, namely, to the effect that the vicar general cannot authorize the erection of a religious house by a clerical institute, must be admitted, if the actual site of the religious house is also approved at the same time.[86] However, if the institute is simply given permission to erect a religious house in an undetermined place, the bishop must intervene and approve the site before the institute can exercise its right to open or construct a church.[87] Hence, the vicar general would not be entirely excluded, at least on the basis of this argument, from competency to authorize even the erection of a clerical religious house.

Goyeneche's second argument, which draws upon the element of analogy, does not seem convincing in the face of the clearly enunciated principles of the Code which define the competency of the vicar general. Canon 198, § 1, states that the vicar general is understood by the term *local ordinary,* unless he is expressly excepted by the law. Furthermore, canon 368, § 1, declares that the vicar general possesses the same ordinary jurisdiction as the bishop of the diocese in all spiritual and temporal affairs, those matters only being excepted which the bishop reserves to himself, or which, by prescript of the law, require a special mandate. Now, the canons governing the erection of religious houses, in demanding the consent of the local ordinary, do not expressly exclude the vicar general from inclusion in this term. Besides, the Code itself provides norms to regulate the prudent conduct of the vicar general and to avoid conflicts between him and the bishop in important matters of curial business. The observance of the norms of canon 369 will prevent any conflict between the vicar general and the bishop in matters of major importance, and the former, if he values his office, will hold fast to these norms.[88]

[86] Can. 497, § 2.

[87] Can. 1162, § 4.

[88] Canon 369, § 1: Vicarius Generalis praecipua acta Curiae ad Episcopum referat, ipsumque certiorem faciat de iis quae gesta aut gerenda sint ad tuendam in clero et populo disciplinam.

The final argument in support of the negative opinion, namely, to the effect that the old law remains unchanged, does not seem to be sustained. Not a few things have been changed by the Code regarding the rights of the vicar general, and, in view of the clearly enunciated principles of canons 198 and 368 in relation to the canons on the erection of religious houses, the matter at issue appears to be one of the things which were changed.[39]

It may be concluded, therefore, that the vicar general is generally competent, by virtue of his ordinary faculties, to permit the erection of a religious house, but that in a special case his competency may be limited either by a special reservation of the bishop or by a conflict with principles stated elsewhere in the Code, as is the case with respect to a clerical religious house in the circumstances previously described.

The competency of the vicar capitular is equally controverted among canonists. Coronata denies that the vicar capitular has the faculty to authorize the erection of a religious house, but gives no reason for his opinion.[40] Chelodi [41] and Melo [42] assert that it is very doubtful that the vicar capitular can give this permission. Creusen also agrees with this opinion, but is somewhat less positive in his assertion. He states that the vicar capitular ought not to permit the authorization of a religious house by reason of the principle "*sede vacante nihil innovetur,*" but he admits that if the permission were given it would appear to be valid.[43]

§ 2: Caveat ne suis potestatibus utatur contra mentem et voluntatem sui Episcopi, firmo praescripto can. 44, § 2.

[39] Campagna, *Il Vicario Generale del Vescovo,* p. 144.

[40] *Institutiones,* n. 523.

[41] *Ius de Personis iuxta Codicem Iuris Canonici* (2. ed., Tridenti: Libr. Tridentum, 1927), p. 413, note 2.

[42] *De Exemptione Regularium,* The Catholic University of America Canon Law Studies, n. 12 (Washington, D. C.: The Catholic University of America, 1921), p. 122.

[43] "Fondation de Maisons Religieuses,"—*RCR,* XI (1935), 129. Fanfani (*De Iure Religiosorum,* n. 21 sqq.) and Pejška (*Ius Canonicum Religiosorum,* pp. 52 sqq.) also seem to deny the faculty in question to the vicar capitular as well as to the vicar general, for, although they do not treat the point professedly, they consistently use the word *episcopus* in their commentary on the requisite permission for the erection of religious houses.

The opposite opinion, however, is based on more convincing juridical arguments. It holds that the vicar capitular can authorize the erection of religious houses, as often as the act does not involve a change in the status of the diocese, or prejudice the rights of the succeeding bishop. This opinion is supported by Schaefer,[44] Larraona,[45] Oesterle [46] and Goyeneche.[47] It is based on the law of the Code that the vicar capitular has ordinary episcopal jurisdiction in all matters excepting those which the law expressly excludes from his competency.[48] The canons on the erection of religious houses do not except the vicar capitular from competency by denying him the faculty to permit their canonical erection. On the other hand, canons 435, § 3, and 436 prescribe adequate norms for the protection of the rights of the diocese and the future bishop.[49] They forbid the vicar capitular to do anything which will prejudice these rights. It cannot be stated as a general principle, however, that every foundation of a religious house will do harm to the diocese or its future bishops. This is a matter which will have to be judged in each particular case, in accordance with the nature and circumstances of the foundation.

The usual interpretation of canon 436 is based on an analogy by which the relationship between the vicar capitular and the diocese is compared to that which exists between tutor and ward. The vicar capitular must not undertake anything which will substantially harm the diocese or the rights of the next bishop, but he may conduct business that will accrue to the benefit of the diocese.[50] Thus, if he foresees that the establishment of a religious house will not only not be harmful, but may even be directly beneficial to the diocese, canon

[44] *De Religiosis,* n. 88, p. 141.

[45] "Commentarium Codicis,"—*CpR,* V (1924), 424.

[46] *Praelectiones Iuris Canonici,* I, 249.

[47] "Consultationes,"—*CpR,* I (1920), 116.

[48] Can. 435, § 1.

[49] Can. 435, § 3: Vicario Capitulari . . . non licet agere quidpiam quod vel dioecesi vel episcopalibus iuribus praeiudicium aliquod afferre possit. . . .

Can. 436: Sede vacante nihil innovetur.

[50] Cf. Coronata, *Institutiones,* n. 461; Connolly, *The Canonical Erection of Parishes,* The Catholic University of America Canon Law Studies, n. 114 (Washington, D. C.: The Catholic University of America, 1938), p. 49.

436 will not of itself prevent him from giving the requisite permission. It could well happen that the grave need of providing more adequate care for souls is too urgent to be postponed until the next bishop arrives.

Hence one may conclude that the vicar capitular has ordinary jurisdiction to authorize the erection of a religious house, but this power may not be exercised in a particular case, if there is danger of injuring the rights of the diocese or its future bishops, or of violating the principle that nothing shall be changed during the vacancy of a see. Naturally, elementary prudence will demand that the vicar capitular refrain from authorizing the erection of a new religious house, unless there be a case of necessity. But if he should see fit to give permission, even outside the case of urgent need, the act of canonical erection would most probably be valid.

Article 2. Authorization in Particular

A. House of a Diocesan Institute

A diocesan institute is one which, having been erected by a local ordinary, has not yet received either the approval or the decree of praise of the Holy See.[51] The norms which prescribe the authorization requisite to erect the religious house of a diocesan institute are given in canons 495, § 1, and 497, § 1. The first of these canons treats exclusively of diocesan congregations which have been extended to more than one diocese, or at least will be so extended by the erection of a new religious house. Diocesan institutes which are limited to one diocese and wish to erect a house within the confines of that same diocese are not considered in this canon. The legislation of canon 497, § 1, provides for the adequate and necessary authorization in this case.

(1) *Foundations outside the diocese of the motherhouse:* Canon 495, § 1, prescribes that when a new religious house of a diocesan institute is to be erected in another diocese permission must be obtained both from the ordinary of the diocese in which the motherhouse is located and from the ordinary of the place where the new house is to be erected. The words of the text, *in alia dioecesi,* clearly

[51] Can. 488, 3°.

refer to a diocese which is distinct from that in which the motherhouse is located. Canonists disagree, however, as to whether this canon applies only to the first foundation in another diocese, or whether its norms must be observed for each new house which is erected in a diocese to which the diocesan institute has spread.

Prümmer [52] and De Meester [53] contend that the ordinary of the diocese of the motherhouse must consent to each foundation which is made in another diocese. Schaefer,[54] with some hesitancy, also inclines to the same opinion.

These authors base their opinion upon a literal interpretation of the words of the canon, *domos constituere non potest,* and argue that these words must be understood as applying to the erection of all houses in another diocese.

The contrary opinion, however, represents the more common view and is supported by more convincing arguments.[55] Canon 495, § 1, is taken from the Constitution *"Conditae a Christo,"* which decreed that a diocesan institute could not move to another diocese except with the consent of both ordinaries whose dioceses were involved in the transfer.[56] The text of the Constitution clearly reveals that the case for which it intended to provide was that in which a diocesan institute *radiated* to another diocese. This condition is not verified when there is question merely of subsequent foundations in another diocese.

Canon 6, 4°, states that one is not to depart from the old law in case of doubt concerning its agreement with the law of the Code. In accordance with this principle, therefore, the words of canon 495, § 1, *"in alia dioecesi domos constituere non potest,"* must be harmonized with those of the Constitution, *"ad dioeceses alias ne transgrediatur."*

[52] *Manuale Iuris Canonici,* q. 181, p. 238.

[53] *Compendium,* I, 391, note 1.

[54] *De Religiosis,* n. 82, pp. 130-131.

[55] Coronata, *Institutiones,* n. 523; Oesterle, *Praelectiones Iuris Canonici,* I, 245; Berutti, *Institutiones Iuris Canonici,* III, 34; Blat, *Commentarium Textus Codicis Iuris Canonici,* II, *Ius de Religiosis et Laicis* (Romae, 1921), n. 549; Larraona, "Commentarium Codicis,"—*CpR,* V (1924), 327; Creusen, "Fondation de Maisons Religieuses,"—*RCR,* XI (1935), 125.

[56] § 1: ". . . sodalitas quaevis dioecesana ad dioeceses alias ne transgrediatur nisi consentiente utroque ordinario. . . ."—*Fontes,* n. 644.

This opinion is further substantiated by the text and context of canon 495, § 1. The canon demands the permission of the ordinary to whose diocese the institutes repairs for its prospective foundation of a new house *(commigrat)*, and forbids the ordinary from whose diocese the institute sets out *(excedit)* to refuse his consent without grave cause. One can hardly speak of an institute's going forth from one diocese and expanding in another except with reference to the first egress of the institute from the diocese of the motherhouse and its simultaneous and first establishment in another diocese.

Finally, it is to be noted that the erection of religious houses within the limits of one diocese is included in the scope of canon 497, § 1. The last clause of this section of canon 497 applies to diocesan institutes and provides adequate norms for the erection of a religious house by these congregations within the confines of a diocese where they are already established. There is no reason for the Code to legislate in canon 495, § 1, with reference to a case which it later treats adequately in canon 497, § 1.[57]

The ordinary of the diocese which is the site of the motherhouse must give permission for every *first* foundation made by a diocesan institute in another diocese. Thus, if an institute which has its motherhouse in diocese A extends to diocese B, and then later to diocese C, the consent of the ordinary of diocese A is required in each case for the first foundation. This is true even if the religious who are to form the new community are not taken from a house in diocese A, but are drawn from a house in diocese B.

Vermeersch asserts that the permission of the ordinary of diocese B is also necessary if the religious assigned to a new house in diocese C are taken from a community in his diocese.[58] This opinion, however, has no foundation in the Code.[59] Besides, the transfer and assignment of religious is an affair which belongs exclusively to the major superior of the congregation, in accordance with the constitutions. It would make good government of the religious institute

[57] Cf. Larraona, "Commentarium Codicis,"—*CpR*, V (1924), 326-327.

[58] Vermeersch-Creusen, *Epitome*, I, n. 559.

[59] The particular law of the constitutions may perhaps require the consent of this local ordinary.

extremely difficult, if this matter required the approbation of the local ordinary.[60]

The motherhouse of a diocesan institute is that which is the ordinary residence of the major superior and the general council. It must not be confused with the house of origin of the institute, since the two may well be distinct. The constitutions of the institute ordinarily define where the motherhouse is to be located and state the conditions under which this site can be changed. If the constitutions are silent in the matter of transferring the motherhouse to another diocese, the consent of the ordinaries of both dioceses involved in the change appears to be necessary. The ordinary of the diocese in which the motherhouse is located is deprived of certain rights by such a transfer, and the ordinary of the diocese to which the motherhouse is moved not only acquires new rights, but is also assigned new obligations of vigilance and supervision. Neither the loss of rights by one ordinary nor the acquisition of added duties by the other should be brought about except by their mutual consent.[61]

The final clause of canon 495, § 1, states that the ordinary of the diocese of the motherhouse cannot refuse his consent for the erection of a house in another diocese without a grave cause. It is to be noted that for a refusal a just cause is not sufficient; the reason for refusing permission must be a grave or serious one. Generally taken, a grave cause is one which is proportionate to the good which a new foundation will accomplish and, on the other hand, to the harm which the diocese of the motherhouse may suffer as a result of the institute's diffusion to another diocese. Ordinarily, the fact that the local ordinary feels that he needs the religious for the houses in his own diocese does not appear to be a cause sufficiently grave for the refusing of consent. However, one can easily suppose an exceptional case in which the transfer of religious to another diocese would do grave and evident harm to the work of the institute in the diocese of the motherhouse.[62] Thus if the institute did not have

[60] Creusen, "Fondation de Maisons Religieuses,"—*RCR*, XI (1935), 126; Larraona, "Commentarium Codicis,"—*CpR*, V (1924), 328, note 216.

[61] Cf. Schaefer, *De Religiosis*, n. 82, p. 131; Vermeersch-Creusen, *Epitome*, I, n. 559; Larraona, "Commentarium Codicis,"—*CpR*, V (1924), 327, note 212.

[62] Larraona, "Commentarium Codicis,"—*CpR*, V (1924), 328, note 213.

enough members to do justice to the work already undertaken in the diocese of the motherhouse, it is evident that the continuance of this work would be seriously endangered by the transfer of some of these religious to another diocese. Also, if the local ordinary judged that the financial condition of the institute would not permit a division, he would certainly have a grave cause for refusing his consent.

The religious have the remedy of recourse to the Holy See against an arbitrary denial of the required permission by the local ordinary.

(2) *Foundations within the same diocese:* The authorization necessary for the erection of the religious house of a diocesan institute within the confines of the same diocese is expressed in the final clause of canon 497, § 1: *secus satis est Ordinarii venia.* Therefore, unless it is a case of founding a house in territory subject to the Sacred Congregation of the Propagation of the Faith, no other approbation is required than that of the local ordinary within whose diocese the house is to be erected.

B. An Exempt House

An exempt house is the house of a religious institute which is not subject to the jurisdiction of the local ordinary.[63] Institutes whose members profess solemn vows are granted the privilege of exemption by the common law. The members of these institutes together with their houses are exempt from episcopal jurisdiction except in those cases wherein the law provides otherwise.[64] The only exception to this rule are nuns who are not subject to a regular superior. Nuns of this class remain under the jurisdiction of the local ordinary and are subject to him as their ordinary superior in all matters in which the Code gives the local ordinary jurisdiction over monastic nuns.[65]

It is a general principle that religious congregations, that is, institutes of simple vows, do not enjoy the privilege of exemption, unless this favor has been granted them by the Holy See.[66] But whether the privilege of exemption is possessed in virtue of the com-

[63] Can. 488, 2°.

[64] Can. 615.

[65] Cans. 500; 615.

[66] Can. 618, § 1. The Passionists and Redemptorists are notable among congregations which have received this privilege.

mon law or whether it derives from a special grant of the Holy See, it must be understood in every case as being restricted by certain provisions of the canons of the Code. No community established in a diocese is entirely withdrawn from the authority of the local ordinary. The erection of religious houses, in particular, is one of several disciplinary matters, mentioned in the Code, in which religious, even of an exempt institute, cannot act without the intervention of the local ordinary.

Canon 497, § 1, prescribes that both the approbation of the Holy See and the written consent of the local ordinary are necessary for the erection of an exempt religious house. *All* exempt religious houses, that is, non-formal as well as formal houses, are included within the scope of this canon. Non-formal houses, although subject to a special vigilance of the local ordinary, still remain exempt. The houses of lay institutes which enjoy a limited exemption are also included in this legislation.[67]

The Sacred Congregation of Religious is competent to grant the necessary papal approbation. But if the exempt house is to be erected in territory subject to the Sacred Congregation of the Propagation of the Faith, then the permission of that body must also be obtained. In this case a petition for approbation must be directed to both congregations, since the approbation of both is obligatory.[68]

[67] Larraona, "Commentarium Codicis,"—*CpR*, V (1924), 420, note 343.

[68] Larraona, *art. cit.*, p. 423; Coronata, *Institutiones*, n. 523.

It is to be noted that Pope Pius XI (1922-1939) extended the jurisdiction of the Sacred Congregation for the Oriental Church, giving it full and exclusive jurisdiction over the following countries: Egypt and the Peninsula of Sinai, Eritrea and Northern Ethiopia, Southern Albania, Bulgaria, Cyprus, Greece, the Dodecanese Islands, Iran, Iraq, Lebanon, Palestine, Syria, Transjordan, Asiatic Turkey and Thracia subject to Turkey. Consequently in these regions the Sacred Congregation for the Oriental Church possesses—not only for the faithful of the Oriental rite but also for the faithful of the Latin rite, and for their hierarchy, works, institutes and pious associations—all the faculties which the other Sacred Congregations possess for the faithful of the Latin rite outside these territories. This extension of jurisdiction is without prejudice, however, to the right of the Holy Office, and without diminution of the reservations which have previously been made to the Sacred Congregation of the Sacraments, to the Sacred Congregation of Rites, to the Sacred Congregation of Seminaries and Universities and to the Sacred Penitentiary. The erection of a

C. Monasteries of Nuns

The scope of the term *monasterium monialium,* as it is used in canon 497, § 1, is a source of controversy among canonists. It is disputed whether the norm which requires the permission of the Holy See applies solely to the monasteries of nuns who take solemn vows, or whether it relates also to the monasteries of nuns who, by special prescript of the Holy See, take only simple vows. Before any discussion of this point, however, a brief history of the background may be helpful to a better understanding of the point at issue.

The political and social upheaval which followed in the train of the French Revolution prompted the Holy See, during the last century, to modify the rule of life for religious orders of women in Belgium and France. It had been the traditional attitude of the Church up until that time to give juridical recognition only to that form of religious life for women which was observed by the regulars in religious orders. This implied the profession of solemn vows and the observance of the papal cloister. But when the enactments of civil law deprived the monasteries of their legal capacity to hold property, it became practically impossible for nuns to observe the obligations of solemn vows and, at the same time, to support their monasteries. Accordingly the Holy See introduced a modification of the rule of life for these institutes of women religious by decreeing that thenceforth their vows would be recognized as simple and that in the establishing of new foundations the members of these institutes were to take simple vows only.[69]

This legislation was extended to the United States in 1864, when Pope Pius IX (1846-1878) declared that only those vows were to be considered solemn which were taken by the nuns in four monasteries of the Order of the Visitation, located in Georgetown, Balti-

religious house in these regions will therefore require the approbation of the Sacred Congregation for the Oriental Church when it is question of a house which requires papal *beneplacitum.* Cf. Pius XI, litt. apost., "*Sancta Dei Ecclesia,*" 25 mart. 1938—*AAS,* XXX (1938), 154.

[69] Cf. S. C. Ep. et Reg., *Lugdunen.,* 14 iun. 1836—*Coll. S. C. Ep. et Reg.,* p. 72; *Parisien.,* 1 aug. 1838—*ibidem,* p. 86; *Gandaven.,* 24 sept. 1816—*ibidem,* p. 411. Cf. also Schaefer, *De Religiosis,* n. 47, pp. 69 sqq.

more, Mobile and Kaskaskia. All other vows taken by nuns in this country were to be considered simple vows unless they obtained a special indult from the Holy See to make solemn profession.[70]

The Sacred Congregation of Religious, in a decree published June 23, 1923, declared that the legal status of the monasteries of nuns in France and Belgium remains unchanged, even after the promulgation of the Code, in regard to their dependence upon the ordinaries of places.[71] The same decree stated, however, that these women religious are true monastic nuns of pontifical approval and declared that if the members of any of these monasteries desire to pronounce solemn vows and to keep the papal enclosure they may obtain that right from the Holy See.[72]

The present legislation declares in canon 488, 7°, that nuns are women religious of solemn vows or, unless the contrary appears from the nature of the case or from the context, women religious whose vows are normally solemn but which, by special disposition of the Holy See are simple in some regions. Several canonists hold that neither the context of the legislation contained in canon 497, § 1, nor the nature of the matter treated therein provides a basis for a distinction between nuns of solemn vows and nuns whose vows are simple, by special prescript.[73] These authors therefore conclude

[70] This legislation was given in the form of a response, transmitted through the Sacred Congregation of Bishops and Regulars, on Sept. 30, 1864, to the Archbishop of Baltimore, with the mandate that it should be communicated to the other bishops of the country.—S. C. Ep. et Reg., *Americana Votorum,* 2 sept. 1864—*Coll. S. C. Ep. et Reg.,* p. 723; *Archiepiscopo Baltimorensi,* 30 sept. 1864—*ibidem,* p. 735.

[71] S. C. de Relig., decr., 23 iun. 1923—*AAS,* XV (1923), 357.

[72] *Ibidem.* In an instruction dated Feb. 6, 1924, relating to the enclosure of nuns with solemn vows, the Sacred Congregation of Religious stated that several monasteries of nuns in France and Belgium had already taken action to secure this permission—*AAS,* XVI (1924), 96. Several monasteries of nuns in the United States have also received permission to take solemn vows. Cf. Reilly, *The Visitation of Religious,* The Catholic University of America Canon Law Studies, n. 112 (Washington, D. C.: The Catholic University of America, 1930), p. 116, note 4.

[73] Cf. Mothon, *Traité sur l'État Religieux* (Paris, 1922), p. 120, and note 8; Schaefer, *De Religiosis,* n. 47, p. 71; Berutti, *Institutiones Iuris Canonici,* III, 33; Vermeersch-Creusen, *Epitome,* I, n. 560; Wernz-Vidal, *De Religiosis,* n. 72; De Meester, *Compendium,* I, 344.

that the permission of the Holy See is necessary for the canonical erection of the monasteries of all nuns alike. In support of their opinion they refer to the decree of the Sacred Congregation of Religious, issued on June 23, 1923, which declared that the nuns in the monasteries of France and Belgium are true monastic nuns in the sense of canon 488, 7°.[74]

Canonists of equal authority, however, contend that the approval of the Holy See is not required for the erection of monasteries of nuns of simple vows, as long as the foundation is to be made in a place where the special prescription regarding simple vows is in force.[75] According to the canonists who hold this opinion the purpose of canon 497, § 1, in demanding papal approbation for the erection of monasteries of nuns is not verified in the case of foundations made by nuns of simple vows. These authors assert that the code requires papal permission for the erection of monasteries of nuns in order to give juridical status to the papal enclosure which nuns of solemn vows must observe. Since monasteries of nuns who pronounce only simple vows are not subject to the prescriptions and sanctions of the papal cloister, these authors contend that the approval of the Holy See is not required for their canonical erection. They argue, moreover, that these monasteries of nuns of simple vows were subject to the local ordinary in pre-Code law, and that the decree of the Sacred Congregation of Religious of June 23, 1923, did not change anything with regard to this dependence but simply declared these women religious to be true monastic nuns. Hence they conclude that the erection of these monasteries in which the nuns profess simple vows is a matter in which the local ordinary is fully competent.

On the basis of these arguments Larraona concludes that, until the contrary is clearly and authentically declared, it may be held as a solid and truly probable opinion that nuns of simple vows need only the permission of the local ordinary to erect a monastery in a place which is subject to the special disposition of the Holy See

[74] S. C. de Relig., decr., 23 iun. 1923—*AAS,* XV (1923), 357.

[75] Cf. Larraona, "Commentarium Codicis,"—*CpR,* V (1924), 421; Maroto, "Annotationes,"—*CpR,* II (1921), 168; Creusen, "Fondation de Maisons Religieuses,"—*RCR,* XI (1935), 127-128; Jombart, "Les Moniales à Voeux Simples,"—*Nouvelle Revue Théologique,* LI (1924), 197 sqq.

regarding the matter of profession with only simple vows.[76] The competent local ordinary in this case will be the ordinary of the place where the monastery is to be erected.[77]

It is to be noted that the discussion thus far has been limited to the case wherein nuns of simple vows wish to erect a monastery in a place subject to the special prescription of the Holy See. The reason for this qualification is that a response of the Sacred Congregation of Religious has clarified the meaning of canon 497, § 1, with regard to the erection of a monastery by these nuns in places which are subject to the common law legislation.[78]

On the basis of this response and the legislation of canon 497, § 1, the following conclusions pertinent to the erection of monasteries by nuns may be regarded as certain:

1. Nuns of *simple* vows need the permission of the Holy See to erect a monastery in a place where the special prescript is *not* in force. Thus, for example, if a community of nuns in France wished to found a monastery of their institute in Italy, papal approbation would be necessary.

2. Nuns of *solemn* vows need the permission of the Holy See to erect a monastery in a place where the special prescript *is* in force. Hence, if a community of nuns in Italy wished to make a foundation in France or Belgium, the consent of the Holy See would be necessary.

3. Nuns of *solemn* vows who wish to erect a monastery in a place subject to the common law legislation need papal approbation. Thus, if a community of nuns in Italy wished to establish a house elsewhere in Italy or in Spain, they would need the permission of the Holy See.

The only situation which this response does not include is that discussed above—the case in which nuns of simple vows desire to make a foundation in a place where the special prescript prevails. As previously noted in the exposition of the contrary opinions concerning the necessity of papal approbation for this case, the weight

[76] "Commentarium Codicis,"—*CpR,* V (1924), 422.

[77] What is to be thought of this view will be indicated later in this discussion.

[78] S. C. de Relig., resp., 11 oct. 1922—*AAS,* XIV (1922), 554.

of canonical authority is evenly divided on both sides of the controversy. The present writer inclines to the opinion which requires the consent of the Holy See for the canonical erection of monasteries by any community of true monastic nuns.

It cannot be proved that the reason in view of which the law demands papal approbation for the erection of monasteries of nuns is conditioned by the establishment of the papal cloister. On the contrary, the history of the legislation on religious houses reveals that other factors prompted the enactments which decreed the necessity of papal approval for the erection of houses by all religious of regular observance. The desire of the Holy See to provide a means of centralized control over the growth of these institutes and to safeguard the vigor of religious life and discipline were the more important motives behind this legislation.

Moreover, the fact that the Holy See by the decree of June 23, 1923, has declared the nuns of France and Belgium to be subject to the local ordinary is not a convincing argument to prove that the local ordinary has also the right to approve the erection of monasteries by these nuns. It must be noted that the decree declares these monasteries to be subject to the ordinaries of places *in those matters in which the Code gives bishops jurisdiction over monastic nuns.*[79] Nowhere, however, does the Code state that the local ordinary is competent to approve the erection of a monastery of nuns. Furthermore, the many decrees and indults of the Sacred Congregation of Bishops and Regulars, issued during the years following the special prescript enjoining simple vows, and previous to the adoption of the Code, clearly indicate that the Holy See did not accord juridical recognition to monasteries of nuns unless they had been established by papal permission.[80] These decrees made no distinction between nuns of solemn vows and those whose vows were simple by special prescript. Hence, there seems to be no true juridical basis for the argument that these nuns of simple vows are now, after the Code, excepted from the general legislation which requires papal approbation for the erection of *monasteries of nuns.*

Finally, it is clear that whatever the merits of this theoretical

[79] S. C. de Relig., 23 iun. 1923—*AAS,* XV (1923), 357.

[80] Cf. the historical section of this work, page 15.

dispute, the permission of the Holy See will be necessary in practice for at least the great majority of cases in which a monastery of nuns is to be established. This necessity is dictated by a related canon of the Code which has a direct bearing upon the point at issue. This canon is number 632, which states that a religious cannot transfer from one institute to another, or go from one independent monastery to another which is equally independent, without the permission of the Holy See.[81] A response of the Sacred Congregation of Religious has declared that the legislation of canon 632 must be observed in the case of nuns of simple vows.[82]

Now, it may be argued that the permission to erect a monastery and the authorization for nuns to transfer to that monastery are two distinct actions. Technically and theoretically this is true. But in practice the canonical erection of a religious house involves the establishment of a collegiate moral person, and, when there is question of the erection of an independent monastery, this moral person, which is the community, cannot be canonically established by taking nuns from another equally independent monastery, on the sole authority of the local ordinary. The erection of the religious house, therefore, necessarily involves the transfer of nuns. Hence, it may be said that, at least in the case wherein two independent monasteries are involved, papal approbation is necessary for the erection of a religious house by nuns of simple vows.

D. Houses in Territory Subject to the Sacred Congregation of the Propagation of the Faith

The places which are subject to the Sacred Congregation of the Propagation of the Faith are generally defined in canon 252, § 3. They are those places where either the hierarchy is not yet established, or, if it is established, is still in its initial stage. In particu-

[81] An independent monastery is one whose internal government is autonomous, that is, independent of any religious superior other than the local superior of the institute. The monasteries of nuns are for the most part independent, even though the authority of the abbess or prioress is very limited in some points by the power accorded to the local ordinaries and regular superiors upon whom the nuns depend. Cf. Creusen-Garesché-Ellis, *Religious Men and Women in the Code*, n. 33.

[82] S. C. de Relig., resp. 9 nov. 1926—*AAS*, XVII (1926), 490.

lar, the list of regions subject to this Congregation is given in the *Annuario Pontificio*.

The permission of the Holy See, accorded through the Sacred Congregation of the Propagation of the Faith, and the written consent of the local ordinary are required for the erection of *any* religious house in these mission regions. There must be question, however, of the erection of a true religious house. Very often religious in mission territories occupy houses which are not true religious houses and are not intended to be such. Thus, two or three members of a community may be sent to direct schools, infirmaries or mission stations, but remain attached to a larger community whose superior is also their proper and immediate local superior.[83] These houses may be erected with the sole authorization of the local ordinary.[84] A papal approbation is required for only those religious houses which form a true and distinct community, subject to its proper superior and stably established for the purpose of carrying out the works proper to the religious institute.[85]

It also frequently happens in mission territories that the prefect or vicar apostolic establishes schools, orphanages, clinics, quasi-parishes, etc., and then requests the members of a religious institute to direct them. These edifices are not religious houses simply by reason of the work which the religious perform in them.[86] Consequently, unless a true religious community with its own proper superior is to be established in the place, no further authorization is necessary.

The encyclical letter of the Sacred Congregation of the Propagation of the Faith on December 7, 1901, implies that the reason for demanding papal approbation for the erection of religious houses in mission territories is the desire of the Holy See for an orderly and uniform régime with respect to religious life in these regions.[87]

[83] Cf. Schaefer, *De Religiosis*, n. 80, p. 127; Vermeersch-Creusen, *Epitome*, I, n. 560.

[84] Cf. can. 497, § 3.

[85] Cf. Schaefer, *loc. cit.* Cf. also page 25 of this work.

[86] Berutti, *Institutiones Iuris Canonici*, III, 33; Wernz-Vidal, *De Religiosis*, n. 71.

[87] S. C. Prop. Fide, litt. encycl., 7 dec. 1901—*ASS*, XXXIV (1901-1902), 639. Cf. also Augustine, *Religious and Laymen*, p. 88.

E. Other Religious Houses

The final clause of canon 497, § 1, expresses the authorization required for the canonical erection of all religious houses which are not explicitly enumerated in the first clause of the canon. Hence, a religious house, which is not exempt, or is not a monastery of nuns, or is not to be located in a territory subject to the Sacred Congregation of the Propagation of the Faith, needs only the authorization of the local ordinary for its canonical erection.

More in particular, the consent of the local ordinary will be requisite but at the same time sufficient in the following cases:

1. When a diocesan institute wishes to erect a religious house in the same diocese as that in which the motherhouse is located.

2. When a diocesan institute, which has been extended to more than one diocese, wishes to establish a house within the confines of any one of these dioceses wherein it is already established.[88]

3. When an insitute of pontifical approval, which is not exempt, wishes to erect a house in any diocese.[89]

The local ordinary in each of these instances is the ordinary of the place where the religious house is to be erected. The common law does not require any permission from the ordinary of the diocese where the motherhouse of a pontifical institute is located, when the foundation is to be made in another diocese.[90]

The norms outlined in the foregoing paragraph suffer an exception when there is question of the erection of a house of novitiate by a pontifical institute. Canon 554, § 1, states that a novitiate must be established according to the norms of the constitutions,

[88] As previously noted, this is the more common and probable opinion. Cf. page 62 of this work.

[89] It may be noted that the Sacred Congregation of Religious has declared that the Congregation of the Sisters of Mercy, whether united under one central government, or having separate houses under the jurisdiction and authority of the local ordinary, is an institute of pontifical approval.—S. C. de Relig., declaratio, 24 nov. 1925—*AAS,* XVIII (1926), 14.

[90] The prescription of the *Normae* of 1901 in this regard must be kept in mind as a guide. No institute of simple vows may petition the local ordinary to authorize the erection of a religious house, unless the general or provincial superior has obtained the consent of his council by a definitive vote. Cf. *Normae* of 1901, art. 305.

and, if the institute in question is of pontifical approval, the permission of the Holy See is necessary. The consent of the ordinary of the place where the novitiate is to be located is also required, in virtue of canon 497, § 1.

In connection with the erection of a novitiate it may also be remarked here that when an institute is divided into provinces there may be only one house of novitiate in each province. A grave reason and a special papal indult are necessary to permit the erection of more than one novitiate house in each province.[91] The grave reason may derive from such factors as the difference of language among the members of the institute, the large territorial extent of the province, or the fact that the province is spread out over more than one country.[92]

If an institute is not divided into provinces, then it appears that the erection of more than one novitiate house is not forbidden, since there is no canon which declares such a prohibition. It is sufficient to have the requisite permission of the Holy See for each house of novitiate, but no special indult is necessary.[93]

Article 3. Formality to Be Observed When the Requisite Authorization Is Sought

The Code does not concern itself with the details which the competent religious superior is to observe in seeking the requisite permission to erect a religious house. It does not specifically determine who is to draw up the petition, nor does it declare, in the event that both papal and episcopal approbation are required, which of these authorizations is to be sought first.

With regard to the first point, the very nature of the matter seems to demand that the petition be directed to the local ordinary and, if the case requires, to the proper congregation of the Holy See by the religious superior who, according to the constitutions, is competent to accept and act upon the institute's officially declared de-

[91] Can. 554, § 2.

[92] Bakalarczyk, *De Novitiatu*, The Catholic University of America Canon Law Studies, n. 36 (Washington, D. C.: The Catholic University of America, 1927), p. 107.

[93] Bakalarczyk, *loc. cit.*

sire to establish a new foundation. There is no reason, however, for which the petition to the Holy See may not be drawn up by the local ordinary, especially if he is also the founder of the new religious house.[94]

With respect to the formality of precedence, canon 497, § 1, gives no certain solution. Pejška believes that the permission of the Holy See should be obtained first.[95] The basis of his opinion is the encyclical letter of the Sacred Congregation of the Propagation of the Faith, published in 1901, which declared that local ordinaries were forbidden to authorize the erection of religious houses in a territory subject to this Congregation, without having first obtained its approval.[96] Pejška concludes that the mind of the Legislator appears to be the same with respect to other regions as well, and that the local ordinary, although he may enter into preparatory discussions with the religious superiors, should not give formal and definite approbation until the permission of the Holy See has been obtained.[97]

Wernz (1842-1914)-Vidal (1867-1938), on the contrary, assert that the local ordinary's permission ought to be sought first.[98] Coronata is even more positive in his assertion to the same effect, stating that the Holy See does not give its permission unless the written permission of the local ordinary is enclosed with the petition.[99]

However, the apparent conflict between the opinion of these last named authors and that of Pejška can readily be harmonized. The deference which is due the Holy See demands that a local ordinary should refrain from granting formal approbation for the erection of a religious house until the requisite consent of the proper congregation of the Roman Curia has been obtained. But, on the other hand, the logical procedure for the erection of a religious house re-

[94] Pejška, *Ius Canonicum Religiosorum*, p. 51.

[95] *Loc. cit.*

[96] "... Diligenter ergo in posterum abstineant ordinarii omnes Sacrae Congregationi subiecti a licentia danda religiosis institutis domum aperiendi in territorio propriae iurisdictionis, absque venia prius a praefata Sacra Congregatione obtenta. . . ." S. C. Prop. Fide, litt. encycl., 7 dec. 1901—*ASS*, XXXIV (1901-1902), 639; *Fontes*, n. 4938.

[97] *Loc. cit.*

[98] *De Religiosis*, n. 71.

[99] *Institutiones*, n. 523, p. 635, note 4.

quires that an investigation concerning the assurance of financial support for the community should precede the petition for authorization.[100] It is scarcely conceivable that the Sacred Congregation would grant its definite approbation unless it had some documentary evidence to the effect that this prerequisite condition had been fulfilled and that the local ordinary was satisfied concerning the assured financial support of the proposed foundation.[101]

In practice, therefore, it seems that the proper method of procedure should include the following steps in logical order: (1) The competent religious superior confers with the local ordinary and together with him makes the required prudent estimate concerning the necessary financial support of the proposed religious house; (2) The local ordinary gives his consent in the form of a *Nihil Obstat,* stating that he approves the foundation on condition that it also meets with the approval of the Holy See; (3) This tentative approbation of the local ordinary is enclosed with the petition which is directed to the proper congregation of the Roman Curia.[102]

[100] Can. 496.

[101] This assertion is borne out by the very positive statement of Coronata, who, if one judge from the tenor of his words, seems to speak from intimate knowledge of the practice of the Roman Curia.

[102] Frequently the procedure is simplified by reason of the fact that the local ordinary asks the religious to establish the house, in order to assist him in the work to be done in his diocese.

CHAPTER VIII

LEGAL CONSEQUENCES OF AUTHORIZATION

Article 1. Diocesan Institutes

Canon 495, § 2: Si ad dioeceses alias eam propagari accidat, nihil de ipsius legibus mutari liceat, nisi de consensu singulorum Ordinariorum quorum in dioecesibus aedes habeat, salvis iis quae, ad normam, can. 492, § 1, Sedi Apostolicae fuere subiecta.

The legal consequences of the legitimate authorization to erect a religious house are authentically interpreted in canon 497, § 2. Before proceeding to comment on the nature of these legal effects, however, one may appropriately discuss at this point the special norm which canon 495, § 2, imposes as a consequence of the extension of a diocesan institute to other dioceses.

The canon in question prescribes that, when the erection of a religious house by an institute of diocesan approval results in the extension of the institute to more than one diocese, no change may be made in the constitutions of the congregation, unless each ordinary in whose diocese the institute has established houses gives his consent. The necessity of unanimous consent is clearly indicated by the words of the canon, which is a practical application of the canonical principle: those matters which touch each one individually, must be approved by all.[1] A contrary vote, therefore, by one of the local ordinaries involved would prevent any change being made in the constitutions.

It must be noted, however, that certain matters pertaining to the constitutions of a diocesan institute cannot be changed even by a unanimous vote of the local ordinaries. The final clause of canon 495, § 2, expressly declares that those things which the Holy See reserved to itself at the time permission was given the local ordinary

[1] Can. 101, § 1, 2°.

to found the institute may never be changed without papal approval.

When the Holy See is consulted about the establishment of a congregation of diocesan approval, information pertinent to the name, habit, intended work, and rule of life of the proposed institute must be submitted for consideration.[2] If the Sacred Congregation, after due consideration, permits the local ordinary to establish the diocesan institute, these articles which have been submitted may not be changed without permission of the Holy See.[3]

Article 2. Clerical Institutes

> **Canon 497, § 2: Constituendae novae domus permissio facultatem secumfert pro religionibus clericalibus habendi ecclesiam vel publicum oratorium domui adnexum, salvo praescripto can. 1162, § 4, et sacra ministeria peragendi, servatis de iure servandis. . . .**

Authorization to erect a religious house by a clerical institute carries with it the right to have a church or public oratory annexed to the house, (subject, however, to the right of the local ordinary to approve the site), and to celebrate the sacred functions in conformity with the requirements of the law.

A clerical institute is one in which at least a notable number of the members is endowed with the priesthood; otherwise it is a lay institute.[4] There is a difference of opinion among canonists as to the true sense of the term *plerique* which the Code uses to define a clerical institute. Schaefer contends that the word signifies the greater numerical part and that a small number of priests does not suffice to constitute a clerical institute, even if the direction of the institute is reserved to them.[5]

[2] Cf. S. C. de Relig., *Normae secundum quas Sacra Congregatio de Religiosis in Novis Congregationibus Approbandis procedere solet,* 6 mart. 1921—*AAS,* XIII (1921), 312-319.

[3] Cf. can. 492, § 1.

[4] Can. 488, 4°: . . . religio cuius *plerique* sodales sacerdotio augentur.

[5] *De Religiosis,* n. 51, p. 78.

Coronata, on the other hand, asserts that, although the word ordinarily signifies the major part, it is not improbable that it may be taken here in the sense of *many*.[6] The opinion of Fanfani is practically similar. He holds that an institute is clerical if a notable part of the members, in contradistinction to a very few by way of exception, is ordained to the priesthood.[7]

An even more liberal interpretation of the definition of a clerical institute is proposed by Vermeersch.[8] He asserts that the mere number of clerics or laymen is not sufficient to determine the legal character of an institute, and that an institute is clerical, even though it admits lay brothers in greater number than clerics, provided that the former remain subordinate to the latter in the constitution and government of the institute. This opinion, which is also supported by Larraona,[9] appears to be sound and probable, since it is consistent with the fact that there actually exist clerical institutes in which the majority of the members is not ordained.[10]

However, it seems that another factor, besides the government of an institute, is important in determining its legal character. This factor is the principal end or work of the religious institute, which, in the old law, was the criterion according to which the character of an institute was determined. Thus, if the institute was destined primarily and by rule for the performance of those works of the ministry which are proper only to priests, it was considered a clerical institute.[11]

The conclusion seems justified, therefore, that an institute need not have a majority of priests among its membership in order to be classified as a clerical institute. If its government is confided to

[6] *Institutiones*, n. 503.

[7] *De Iure Religiosorum*, n. 5.

[8] Vermeersch-Creusen, *Epitome*, I, n. 542.

[9] "Commentarium Codicis,"—*CpR*, II (1921), 286.

[10] Molitor (*Religiosi Iuris Capita Selecta* [Ratisbonae, 1909], p. 27) cites the Camillists as an example of an institute which has always been included among the clerks regular, but which, by virtue of its constitutions, admits a greater number of lay brothers than clerics to profession.

[11] Appeltern, *Compendium Praelectionum Iuris Regularis* (Parisiis, Tornaci, 1913), q. 25, p. 18.

clerics, and the primary work for which the institute is destined pertains to the sacerdotal state, the institute may be considered clerical.

A. Right to a Church or Public Oratory

> **. . . habendi ecclesiam vel publicum oratorium domui adnexum. . . .**

Churches and oratories are places consecrated to divine worship, but whereas a church is intended to serve all the faithful for the exercise of public worship, an oratory is intended solely, or at least especially, for a determined group of persons.[12] A *public* oratory is one to which all the faithful have the right to come, at least during the hours of services.[13]

According to the common opinion of canonists, the church or public oratory to which clerical institutes have a right, in virtue of canon 497, § 2, need not be materially joined to the religious house. A moral unity between the house and the sacred edifice is sufficient. Such moral unity is had when the church or public oratory is sufficiently adjacent to the religious house that it may be considered to be a formal part of the house and to constitute with it one group of buildings.[14]

It is important to note that the law itself gives to clerical institutes the right to have a church or public oratory attached to a canonically erected house.[15] The permission to erect a house, in the case of these institutes, carries with it a twofold right: the right to erect the house itself, and the faculty of opening or constructing

12 Cans. 1161 and 1188, § 1.

13 Can. 1188, § 2, 1°.

14 Beste, *Introductio in Codicem,* 323; Fanfani, *De Iure Religiosorum,* n. 369; Gerster, *Ius Religiosorum in Compendium Redactum* (Taurini: Marietti, 1935), p. 27; Oesterle, *Praelectiones Iuris Canonici,* I, 246; Larraona ("Commentarium Codicis,"—*CpR,* V [1924], 427) agrees as regards the church, but believes that an oratory should be materially attached to the house, "partim ex rei natura, partim ex legis praescripto."

15 Can. 497, § 2. The religious of a lay institute require the special permission of the local ordinary in order to have a church or a public or semi-public oratory in connection with their religious house. Cf. cans. 1162; 1191, § 1; 1192.

a church or public oratory adjacent to the house. The local ordinary, therefore, may not attach a contrary condition to his permission for the erection of the religious house by stating, for instance, that he approves the establishment of the house, but that he forbids the institute to have a church or public oratory. The text of the law states absolutely that the permission to erect a clerical house implies the faculty of having a church or public oratory. It does not admit any contrary exceptions or conditions, as it does in the case of the exercise of the proper works of the institute. Since the local ordinary cannot derogate the common law, it follows that any condition contrary to it would be invalid.

It appears, however, that the local ordinary may permit only the minimum which the law concedes, namely a public oratory, and exclude the erection of a church. The text of the canon is disjunctive and states that the clerical religious house has the right to a church *or* a public oratory.[16]

But even though the local ordinary may not attach a contrary condition to his consent, the Code itself imposes a condition which, in practice, restricts the use of the right granted by the law to a clerical religious house with respect to a church or public oratory: the local ordinary must approve the site upon which the sacred edifice is to be erected, before the religious may proceed to build.[17]

[16] Larraona, "Commentarium Codicis,"—*CpR,* V (1924), 427; Toso, *Ad Codicem Iuris Canonici Commentaria Minora,* lib. II, pars II, *De Religiosis* (Romae: Marietti, 1927), p. 22. (Hereafter this work is cited as *Commentaria Minora*).

[17] Cans. 497, § 2, and 1162, § 4. But if the local ordinary approves the erection of a clerical religious house on a definite and determined site, e. g., at 110 N. Street, city of N., diocese of N., it seems that no further approval is necessary for the site of an annexed church or public oratory. Since the institute has a right to have a church or public oratory, by prescript of the law itself, the permission of the ordinary to establish the house on a fixed site implicitly includes approbation of that site for the church or oratory. Besides, canon 1162, § 4, states that the religious of a clerical institute need special permission to erect their church or public oratory on a definite site, when they have obtained authorization to establish a house *in a city or a diocese.* This seems to imply that the special approval of the site is required only when the permission to erect the house has been more or less indefinite as regards location, but is not necessary when the definite site has already been fixed. Cf.

Consequently, a local ordinary who does not wish to permit the erection of a church or public oratory by a clerical institute, has a means of obtaining his end. He can let it be known that he will not authorize the erection of the proposed religious house, if the religious intend to use the right conceded to them by canon 497, § 2, or he may refuse to approve the site, chosen by them, for their church or public oratory.

In the first case, the religious may spontaneously renounce the use of their right in order to obtain authorization for the erection of the religious house. With regard to the second alternative, however, it must be emphasized that the local ordinary cannot arbitrarily refuse to approve a site chosen by the religious for their church or oratory. Once the local ordinary has consented to the erection of the house, the religious of a clerical institute obtain an acquired right to a church or public oratory and, consequently, if the ordinary refuses to approve a location for the edifice, without just cause, they may seek a legal remedy against his decision by instituting a judicial action.[18]

The second and third paragraphs of canon 1162 prescribe the norms which a bishop must observe in authorizing the erection of a church, and, at the same time, indicate the reasons for which he would be justified in refusing his approval of the site for a church or a public oratory to be erected by a clerical religious house.[19] It

Berutti, *Institutiones Iuris Canonici,* III, 35; Toso, *Commentaria Minora,* lib. II, pars II, p. 20.

It is to be noted also that canon 1162 considers only the hypothesis of a church which is *to be built.* Hence the canon does not seem to apply if there is question of a church which already exists. The permission to erect a religious house would suffice to make use of an adjacent church or public oratory. Cf. Larraona, "Commentarium Codicis,"—*CpR,* V (1924), 428; Chelodi, *Ius de Personis,* pp. 413-414.

[18] Can. 1667: Quodlibet ius . . . actione munitur. . . .

[19] Can. 1162, § 2: Ordinarius consensum ne praebeat, nisi prudenter praeviderit necessaria non defutura ad novae ecclesiae aedificationem et conservationem, ad ministrorum sustentationem aliasque cultus impensas.

§ 3: Ne nova ecclesia ceteris iam exsistentibus detrimentum afferat, maiore fidelium spiritualium utilitate non compensatum, Ordinarius, antequam consensum praebeat, audire debet vicinarum ecclesiarum rectores quorum intersit, firmo praescripto can. 1676.

is true that canon 497, § 2, does not expressly refer to the second and third paragraphs of canon 1162, but cites only the fourth paragraph. However, the purpose of this fourth paragraph of canon 1162, which requires only the ordinary's approval of the site for the church or oratory and not his consent to build it (which is already had by the clerical institute through the prescript of the law), is obviously to safeguard the observance of the norms of the previous two paragraphs. In other words, the Code requires a special approval, in canon 1162, § 4, of the site for a church or an oratory to be built by a clerical religious house, precisely because the place where a church is to be located is an important factor in determining whether the financial provisions, required by canon 1162, § 2, and the compensation of greater spiritual good, prescribed by canon 1162, § 3, can be assured.

One may conclude, therefore, that if the bishop prudently foresees that the necessary financial support of the proposed religious church cannot be assured, or that other churches in the vicinity will suffer detriment, without adequate compensation in the way of greater spiritual good to the faithful, he will be justified in refusing his approval of the site proposed by the members of a clerical religious house for their church or public oratory.

However, if the conditions prescribed by canon 1162, §§ 2 and 3, are satisfactorily fulfilled, may the bishop still refuse to approve the site chosen by the religious institute? Chelodi believes that the bishop would not be justified in refusing his consent.[20] This opinion appears to be juridically sound, for, since the authorization to erect a clerical religious house gives the institute a *canonical* right to have a church or a public oratory, it seems only consistent that the bishop ought to base his prohibition to exercise this right on a *canonical cause.* It must be remarked, however, that the conditions prescribed by canon 1162 involve a judgment on the part of the bishop. Although this judgment is to be based on norms stated in the law, nevertheless it allows a great measure of freedom to the bishop, and undoubtedly it would be very difficult to prove that his judgment in regard to the advisability of building a church on a certain site is not justified by the facts. In practice, this point will

[20] *Ius de Personis,* p. 414, note 1.

of course be settled by judicial decree, since the religious have the right to recur to the Holy See if they believe that their right to a church or oratory has been unjustly violated.[21]

The interrelationship of canons 497, § 2, and 1162, which has already been demonstrated, also makes it clear that the bishop is obliged, before granting his approval, to consult the rectors of churches which are in the neighborhood of the clerical religious house.

The law does not oblige the bishop to obtain the consent of these rectors, but only demands that he ask their advice. According to the norm of canon 105, 1°, the bishop is not held to act in conformity with this advice, but he should not proceed contrary to the unanimous judgment of the interested rectors, unless he has a prevailing reason. It is neither necessary nor pertinent to the purpose of this work to enter into the controversy which centers around the interpretation of that phrase of canon 105, 1°, which states that, when the law demands consultation, it is sufficient for the validity of the act that the superior consult the persons concerned. Whether the bishop omits entirely to consult the rectors of near-by churches, or whether he acts contrary to their advice, the rights of these rectors and their churches are adequately protected by legal remedy. If they believe that the erection of a new church or public oratory in the neighborhood will prejudice their rights, these rectors may institute the judicial action of *Nuntiatio Novi Operis*.[22]

The institution of this action has the effect of an injunction in civil law, and obliges an immediate interruption of the work on the proposed oratory or church, until the evidence in the case has been presented and the rights of both parties have been decided by judicial sentence.[23]

Both the purpose and the context of canon 1162, § 3, clearly indicate that the term *rectores* must be taken here in a wide sense to include rectors of parish churches, that is pastors, as well as rectors

[21] Can. 1667. Cf. also Melo, *De Exemptione Regularium*, p. 127.

[22] Can. 1676.

[23] However, if adequate steps are taken to insure that matters will be restored to their original status, in the event of an unfavorable decision for the convened party, the judge may allow the continuation of the work. Cf. can. 1676, § 2.

in the strict sense of the term.[24] The purpose of this legislation, as its sources indicate, is to safeguard the rights of all churches established in the vicinity of the clerical religious house.[25] Moreover, the Code obviously uses the word *rectores* in order to make it clear that the rights of all priests in charge of churches, both parochial and non-parochial, are to be respected.[26]

The Code does not specify or define the nature of the detriment which an interested rector must claim to suffer in order to justify his opposition to a proposed church or public oratory. Certainly, the violation of his strictly parochial rights would constitute a just claim. But, since the Code does not restrict the alleged harm to parochial rights, it may be permitted to say that any serious material or pecuniary loss to a church or its rector would appear to be the basis for a judicial action.[27]

It must be emphasized, however, that this detriment must be so grave as not to be compensated by the greater spiritual good of the faithful which will accrue from the opening of the new church. Since this is a matter of judgment on the part of the bishop, it is evident that in practice it will be very difficult for a rector to obtain a favorable decision through judicial action.[28]

Before dismissing this point concerning the right of a clerical religious house to have a church or a public oratory, one may well add that many difficulties and inconveniences, incident to the erection of these sacred edifices, can be avoided by settling the issue at the time permission is asked for the erection of the religious house itself. If the religious intend to have a church or a public oratory attached to the proposed house, they should ask the ordinary for

[24] Can. 479, §1: Nomine rectorum ecclesiarum hic veniunt sacerdotes, quibus cura demandatur alicuius ecclesiae, quae nec paroecialis sit nec capitularis, nec adnexa domui communitatis religiosae, quae in eadem officia celebret.

[25] C. 43, C. XVI, q. 1: Ecclesiae antiquitus constitutae nec decimis, nec ulla possessione priventur, ita ut novis oratoriis tribuantur.

C. 44, C. XVI, q. 1: . . . omnino providendum est episcopo, ut aliae ecclesiae antiquiores propter novas suam iustitiam aut decimam non perdant, sed semper ad antiquiores ecclesias persolvantur.

Cf. also Reiffenstuel, *Ius Canonicum Universum,* lib. III, tit. 48, n. 17.

[26] Coronata, *Institutiones,* n. 732, p. 34, note 1.

[27] Cf. Coronata, *Institutiones,* n. 732. Cf. also cans. 1410 and 463, § 1.

[28] Wernz-Vidal, *De Religiosis,* n. 75, p. 73, note 22.

his approval of the site of their church or oratory at the same time at which they ask his approval for the house itself. This will prevent any difficulties or misunderstandings later on. If this is done, however, it is evident that the local ordinary must consult the rectors of the churches close at hand and observe the other norms prescribed by canon 1162, §§ 2 and 3, before he grants the requisite authorization for the religious house.

B. Right to Celebrate Sacred Functions

. . . et sacra ministeria peragendi, servatis de iure servandis. . . .

Permission to erect a religious house also carries with it, in the case of a clerical institute, the right to perform the sacred functions in accordance with the prescripts of the law. It is apparent from the context of canon 497, § 3, that there is question here of the ordinary works of the sacred ministry, which are the common right and privilege of clerics, in so far as they are to be performed within the church or public oratory of the religious house.[29]

The sacred functions which the religious of a clerical institute may celebrate in their church or public oratory may be generally classified as pertaining to the eucharistic worship, the administration of the sacraments, and the ministry of preaching. Since the Code adds that these functions must be performed with due observance of the requirements of the law, it will be useful to note here the more important prescriptions which must be observed.

General Norms

(1) In a sacred edifice which has been legitimately blessed all ecclesiastical rites may be performed, but the rights of parish churches and the rights acquired by privilege or legitimate custom must be safeguarded. Moreover, except in the case of a church

[29] The last clause of canon 497, § 3, provides for the more general work of the religious institute to be exercised both within and without the limits of the religious house. Cf. Larraona, "Commentarium Codicis,"—*CpR,* V (1924), 429.

which belongs to an exempt institute, the local ordinary may, for a just cause, fix the hours of services in all sacred edifices subject to his jurisdiction. In churches of exempt religious institutes, the local ordinary may not fix the hours of services, but he has the right to decide whether or not the functions celebrated in these churches interfere with the catechetical instruction or explanation of the gospel, which must be given in the parish church.[80]

(2) Public oratories are ruled by the same law as churches. Hence, if a public oratory has been dedicated to the public worship of God with a blessing or a consecration, as authorized by the local ordinary, then all sacred functions can take place, except those which the rubrics do not allow in oratories.[81]

(3) The rector of a religious church can celebrate the divine services in a solemn manner, observing however the laws of the charter of foundation, and provided that there is no interference with the ministry of the parish church. The local ordinary is the judge in these matters and he may lay down opportune norms to avoid confusion.[82]

(4) If a non-parochial church is so far distant from the parish church of the territory that the parishioners who live near the non-parochial church cannot be expected, in the judgment of the local ordinary, to go to the parish church for Mass and other divine services, the parishioners in question may attend the non-parochial church. The local ordinary, moreover, may order the rector of this church to have services at hours convenient to the people, to announce the feast and fast days, and to give catechetical instruction and an explanation of the gospel.[83]

Eucharistic Worship

(1) *Holy Mass.*

(a) In all religious houses which have the faculty of reserving the Blessed Sacrament habitually, one priest may celebrate the three Masses of Christmas, beginning at midnight, or he may say only one

[80] Cans. 1171 and 609, § 3.

[81] Can. 1191, §§ 1-2.

[82] Can. 482.

[83] Can. 483, 1°-2°.

Mass, according to the liturgy of the day. All who are present at this Mass satisfy the precept of hearing Mass, and Holy Communion may be distributed.[84]

(b) The solemn functions of Holy Week may be celebrated in any duly blessed or consecrated church or public oratory, in which the Blessed Sacrament is reserved.[85] If not all the functions of the three days are to be held, one Mass may nevertheless be said on Holy Thursday in the churches and oratories of regulars, and Holy Communion may be distributed.[86]

(c) In a house of exempt religious the major superior may, in a particular case by way of exception and for a just and reasonable cause, allow Mass to be said outside of the church or public oratory, but never in a place which actually serves as a bedroom. Other clerical religious must obtain this permission from their local ordinary.[87]

(2) *Reservation of the Blessed Sacrament.*

(a) Provided that there is someone to take care of the Blessed Sacrament and that Mass is said at least once a week in the church or public oratory, exempt religious are obliged to keep the Blessed Sacrament in the church or public oratory annexed to their house; and with the authorization of the local ordinary it becomes permissible to keep the Blessed Sacrament in the principal oratory of *every* religious house.[88]

(b) In churches or oratories for which it is allowed to keep the Blessed Sacrament, private exposition, that is with the ciborium, is

[84] Can. 821, § 3. Bishops in the United States have the power, in virtue of their quinquennial faculties, to grant this permission to other religious churches not indicated in canon 821, § 3. Cf. the faculties from the Sacred Congregation of Religious—Bouscaren, *The Canon Law Digest, Supplement—1941* (Milwaukee: Bruce, 1941), p. 32, n. 2.

[85] S. R. C., *Neapolitana*, 14 iun. 1659—*Decreta Authentica Congregationis Sacrorum Rituum* (Romae, 1898-1927), I, n. 1120. (Hereafter this collection is cited as *Decr. Auth.*).

[86] S. R. C., *Comen.*, 9 dec. 1899—*Decr. Auth.*, n. 4049. The quinquennial faculties of bishops in the United States permit them to grant this privilege to any religious community. Cf. the faculties from the Sacred Congregation of Religious—Bouscaren, *The Canon Law Digest, Supplement of 1941*, p. 32, n. 7.

[87] Can. 822, § 4.

[88] Can. 1265, § 1, 1°, 2°.

permissible for any just reason without the consent of the local ordinary. On the Feast of Corpus Christi and during its octave, it is allowed to expose the Blessed Sacrament publicly, that is, in the monstrance, during solemn Mass and Vespers; to do so at other time, a grave cause is required and permission must be had from the local ordinary, even in the case of exempt religious.[39]

(c) The public exposition of Forty Hours is obligatory for all public oratories in which the Blessed Sacrament is reserved.[40]

Ministry of Preaching

(1) For preaching to exempt men religious, or to those who live steadily at their house as students, guests, convalescents or servants, the faculty of preaching is granted in a clerical institute by that superior whom the constitutions specify. But for preaching to non-exempt men in a clerical institute the faculty of preaching is granted by the local ordinary even to the priest members of that institute.[41]

(2) The faculty to preach to lay people other than those who reside day and night in the house of an exempt clerical institute may be given only by the local ordinary. Hence, clerical religious may not preach at public services in the church or public oratory of their religious house without having obtained the requisite faculty from the local ordinary.[42]

Administration of Sacraments

(1) *Baptism.*

The local ordinary may, for the convenience of the faithful, permit or order that a baptismal font be placed in another church or public oratory within the territorial limits of a parish. But even though a religious non-parochial church may have a baptismal font, the pastor's rights must be respected. Only the pastor has the right to confer solemn baptism and to bless the baptismal font on Holy Saturday.[43]

[39] Can. 1274, § 1.

[40] Can. 1275.

[41] Can. 1338, §§ 1-2.

[42] Cans. 1337 and 1338, § 2.

[43] Cans. 774, § 2; 775; 462, 1°, 7°.

(2) *Holy Communion.*

(a) Holy Communion may be distributed wherever it is permitted to say Mass, unless the local ordinary, for a just cause, prohibits it in a particular case.[44]

(b) Holy Communion may be distributed during Mass every day except Good Friday. It may be distributed, as a general rule, only during the hours when Mass may be celebrated, but a reasonable cause is sufficient to distribute it at any other time.[45]

(c) Holy Communion, when it is to be received by reason of devotion, may be brought to the sick of a religious house by any priest, with at least the presumed permission of the priest who has custody of the Blessed Sacrament.[46] However, if a priest other than the pastor of the place brings Holy Communion to a sick member of the religious house, he must do so privately, for the right of carrying the Blessed Sacrament publicly to the sick belongs to the pastor within his own territory. Other priests may exercise the right only in cases of necessity and with at least the presumed permission of the pastor or the local ordinary.[47]

(3) *Viaticum and Extreme Unction.*

In every clerical institute superiors have the right and duty of administering the sacraments of Viaticum and Extreme Unction to the sick who are professed members or novices of the community, or who live day and night in the religious house, by reason of employment, education, hospitality or infirmity.[48]

[44] Can. 869.

[45] Can. 867, §§ 1, 2, 4.

[46] Can. 849, § 1. If the Blessed Sacrament is taken from the tabernacle of the church or oratory attached to the religious house, the presumed permission of the religious who has charge of the church or oratory will be necessary (cans. 1269, § 4; 415, § 3, 1°). However, if the priest to whom the care of the church or oratory has been committed is other than the superior of the house, the permission of the latter is not required, according to the common law at least, in order to bring Communion to a member of the community.

[47] Can. 848, §§ 1, 2. Cf. Fanfani, *De Iure Religiosorum*, n. 418.

Allowance must be made, however, for the possible application of the potential norm indicated in canon 464, § 2. For a just and grave cause, the bishop may withdraw religious houses within the territory of a parish from the care of the pastor.

[48] Can. 514, § 1.

(4) *Penance.*

(a) The superior of a clerical exempt institute, according to the norms of the constitutions, has ordinary jurisdiction. He may consequently delegate faculties to hear the confessions of the professed religious of the community as well as of the novices and others who live day and night in the religious house.[49]

(b) Confessors in a clerical non-exempt religious house must receive faculties from the local ordinary, even to hear the confessions of the members of their own community.[50]

(c) All clerical religious must obtain faculties from the local ordinary to hear the confessions of the laity, of the secular clergy and of the religious of other institutes, even of nuns subject to them, who come to their church or public oratory.[51]

(5) *Celebration of Marriage.*

Marriage between Catholics is to be celebrated in the parish church. It may be celebrated in the church or public oratory of a religious institute only with the permission of the local ordinary or the proper pastor.[52]

Funeral Services

(1) The funeral services of a deceased religious are to be held in the church or oratory of his own religious house, or at least in a church or oratory of his institute.[53]

(2) If a religious dies far away from his religious house, so that the body cannot be conveniently transported to the church or oratory of his house, or at least to a church of his institute, the funeral services shall take place in the church of the parish where he died. However, the religious superior always has the right to bring the body of the deceased, at his own expense, to a church of the institute.[54]

(3) Novices are treated like professed religious in this matter,

[49] Cans. 873, § 2, and 875, § 1.

[50] Can. 875.

[51] Cans. 874, § 1; 525.

[52] Can. 1109, § 1.

[53] Can. 1221, § 1.

[54] Can. 1221, § 2.

unless they have chosen, as they have a right, to be buried from some particular church.[55]

(4) Servants who work for the religious community and live habitually within the confines of the religious house are treated as novices with regard to burial, if they die in the house; but if they die outside of the religious house, they are buried as the rest of the faithful.[56]

(5) Funeral services of clerical religious who are entitled by law to be buried from an oratory or church of their own institute are to be conducted by the proper religious superior.[57]

Article 3. All Religious Institutes

> . . . pro omnibus religionibus, pia opera exercendi religionis propria, salvis conditionibus in ipsa permissione appositis.

The final effect of authorization to erect a religious house is the right acquired by the religious to carry on the works which are proper to the rule of their institute. By the term *pia opera* is understood the various ministries of the active life which are the particular end or aim of the religious institute in question. These works will naturally vary according to the nature of the institute and its fundamental rule of life, and will include such diverse works as the education of youth, the nursing of the sick, engaging in parish work or missionary activity, and caring for the poor, the orphaned or the aged.[58]

The right of a legitimately established religious house to carry on its proper works may be said to derive from the very nature of

[55] Can. 1221, §§ 1-2.

[56] Can. 1221, § 3.

[57] "Generale principium quo ecclesiae funerantis rector ministro funerum fungitur totam suam vim obtinet pro religiosis."—Coronata, *Institutiones*, n. 805. Cf. cans. 1221, § 1, and 514, § 4.

[58] It may also be noted here that permission to erect a religious house implies the right to establish in the house or adjacent church any lay association or society which is proper to the institute and which is not organized as an organic body, that is, one which is not established as a distinct moral person, according to the norm of canon 100. Cf. can. 686, § 3.

the act of canonical erection. The establishment of a religious house would be entirely lacking in purpose, if the religious were not permitted to perform the very works for which their institute has been founded. However, the text of canon 497, § 2, clearly indicates that the local ordinary may limit the exercise of these works by attaching certain conditions to his permission for establishing a religious house. In a diocese where there are many religious institutes, good order will often demand that the local ordinary impose such conditions. For instance, he may restrict the work of an institute, which does both teaching and nursing, to the ministry of the sick in this particular house; he may limit the work of the religious to the faithful of a certain nationality, or permit them to have a school of only elementary grades.[59] However, the conditions imposed must not be contrary to the common law rights and privileges of the religious institute, or to the particular law of their constitutions which have been approved by the Holy See. Furthermore, the restrictions should not be such as to exclude altogether the primary work for which the institute is destined by rule and foundation.[60]

In general, a just reason for imposing limitations of this kind is the desire on the part of the local ordinary to provide for all the needs of his diocese in a fair and equitable manner, and, at the same time, to avoid harmful competition and rivalry between religious institutes and between them and the secular clergy.

If the local ordinary desires to impose restrictions upon the work to be carried on by the members of a new religious house, he should make certain that these limitations are specifically and exhaustively expressed in the permission to establish the house. This specification is necessary not only that the restrictions may have legal binding force, but also as a measure of precaution to avoid future discord and misunderstanding. Once a local ordinary has authorized the establishment of a religious house, he may not afterward add conditions which limit the work of the religious. These

[59] Beste, *Introductio in Codicem,* 323; Farrell, *The Local Ordinary and Women Religious of Pontifical Approval,* p. 62.

[60] Larraona, "Commentarium Codicis,"—*CpR,* V (1924), 430; Oesterle, *Praelectiones Iuris Canonici,* I, 247.

conditions are considered in law as non-existent, unless they are attached to the act of consent requisite for the erection of the religious house. For canon 497, § 2, clearly and emphatically states that permission to erect a religious house gives to all religious institutes the right to carry out their proper works, unless conditions limiting this right are *attached to the permission itself.*

CHAPTER IX

EDIFICES SEPARATE FROM THE RELIGIOUS HOUSE

Canon 497, § 3: Ut aedificentur et aperiantur schola, hospitium vel similis rationis aedes separata a domo etiam exempta, necessaria est et sufficit specialis Ordinarii scripta licentia.

Article 1. Scope of the Law

The authorization prescribed by the first paragraph of canon 497 is required only for the erection of a religious house in the strict sense of the term.[1] It frequently happens, however, that the religious of a particular religious house desire to extend the scope of their activity by opening or constructing a school, hospice or similar edifice in connection with their religious house. If the work to be undertaken in the proposed edifice is proper to the institute, and in the permission to erect the religious house no limitation was imposed concerning this particular work, then, according to the norm of canon 497, § 2, the religious have a right to this extension of their activity. However, paragraph 3 of this same canon adds a condition restricting this right: the new work must be undertaken in a building which is not separate from the religious house. Hence, if the extention of the proper work of the institute is going to involve the opening or construction of a building separate from the religious house, a special written permission of the local ordinary is required, that is, a permission which is distinct from that which was given for the religious house of which this edifice is to constitute a formal part. This special written permission is necessary for the opening or construction of separate edifices by any type of religious institute, and it suffices even when an exempt institute is involved. The new building, since it is a part of the exempt religious house, will share in its privilege of exemption.[2]

[1] Cf. pages 25 and 36 of this work.

[2] Can. 615.

The term *schola* must be taken here in a general sense to include educational institutes of every classification—elementary, secondary or collegiate—which are opened or erected in an edifice separate from an established religious house.[3] However, Melo [4] and Toso [5] restrict the scope of the term to schools which are intended for the education of the lay faithful. They hold that an apostolic school is not subject to the prescript of canon 497, § 3. This opinion seems tenable if the apostolic school in question is to be used solely for the training of postulants of the religious institute, and is not at the same time the residence of a religious community. The education of aspirants to the religious life is a work which is not only proper to every religious institute, but is confined within the institute itself. The purpose of canon 497, § 3, on the other hand, and the connotation of the Constitution "*Romanos Pontifices,*" which is the source of this legislation, indicate that the edifices included within the scope of this law are those which exert an external influence on the clergy or laity.[6] These are edifices opened or constructed by the religious institute for the purpose of carrying out the spiritual and corporal works of mercy, such as the education of youth, the care of the sick and the orphaned, and the provision of shelter for travelers. The education and training of postulants can hardly be included in the same category as these other works, since it is a work which pertains exclusively to the internal order of a religious institute.

It must be remarked, however, that an apostolic school which is open to extern students as well as to prospective candidates for the religious life will be included within the scope of canon 497, § 3, since in this case the interests of the laity and secular clergy are clearly involved. The same is also true of an apostolic school, even of one exclusively intended for postulants, which is used as the permanent residence for the religious serving as teachers. In this latter case the building will come under the legislation of canon 497, § 3, not because it is a school, but because it is the residence of a

[3] Schaefer, *De Religiosis,* n. 86, p. 135, note 6; Beste, *Introductio in Codicem,* p. 326.

[4] *De Exemptione Regularium,* p. 128.

[5] *Commentaria Minora,* lib. II, pars II, *De Religiosis,* p. 22.

[6] Cf. Blat, *De Religiosis,* n. 73; Melo, *loc. cit.*

group of religious. As such it must be erected at least as a branch or filial house.

In further exposition of the term *schola* it must also be pointed out that the situation contemplated by this canon is that in which the school depends upon and is attached to an established house. A much different situation occurs when a school is established by a parish or diocese and the religious are simply engaged to serve as teachers. In this case there is no question of acquisition of the school by the religious, and consequently the special written permission, prescribed by canon 497, § 3, is not necessary in order that the religious may undertake this work. However, if the religious house from which the teachers are drawn is so far distant from the school in question that the religious appointed to teach must take up residence in or near the school, then permission will be necessary for another reason, namely, for the establishment of a filial religious house.

A hospice, in the strict sense, is a guest house, that is, a residence established for the purpose of affording rest and shelter to travelers. In the particular law of many religious institutes, however, the term is used in a wider sense to include villas, rural houses inhabited by a small group of religious who supervise the community farm, retreat houses and residences intended for the use of members of the institute who are pursuing advanced study.[7] This diversity of application of the term makes it clear that the mere title of *hospice* will not always be sufficient to determine whether or not a house which bears that name, by virtue of particular law or custom, is to be included within the scope of canon 497, § 3.

Pre-Code doctrine distinguished hospices which were intended primarily to provide shelter for pilgrims and in which there was no observance of the regular discipline from hospices, improperly so-called, in which the regular discipline was observed. A special permission of the local ordinary was necessary but also sufficient to establish the former type of hospice, but the latter required the full solemnities of a canonical erection.[8]

[7] Cf. Augustine, *Religious and Laymen*, p. 92; Oesterle, *Praelectiones Iuris Canonici*, I, 247.

[8] Benedictus XIV, *De Synodo Dioecesana*, lib. IX, cap. 1, n. 9; Appeltern, *Compendium Praelectionum Iuris Canonici*, q. 657, p. 591.

Hospices of both these types continue to exist at the present time. According to the present discipline, however, the pre-Code distinction is not entirely adequate to determine the formalities which are required by law for the opening or construction of a house bearing the title of hospice, for not only the purpose of the house, but its legal status with regard to other houses of the same institute, must be taken into consideration. As will be demonstrated more fully in Article 2 of this Chapter, the special written permission, prescribed by canon 497, § 3, is sufficient only for the establishment of a strictly filial religious house. Consequently, a hospice may be opened or erected in accordance with the norm of canon 497, § 3, only when it is to be a dependent house of strictly filial character. On the other hand, if a hospice is to be established with its proper community and religious superior, the complete formalities of a canonical erection must be observed, even though the particular law of the institute involved may use the term hospice in reference to the house.[9]

Finally, it is to be noted that houses which are to be used for merely secular purposes and in which no permanent community is to reside do not require even this special written permission of the local ordinary. Thus, villas, farmhouses, hostels, which are intended solely as places of rest and shelter for members of the religious institute, and other similar buildings, are not included within the scope of canon 497, § 3. It is clear from the context of this law that it is concerned only with edifices which fall within the classification of religious houses in at least the wide sense, that is, of houses in which the religious live *as religious*.[10] Only in the rare instance that the religious institute intends to use these residences for religious as well as purely secular purposes, by carrying out some of its proper works in connection with them, will it be necessary to observe the prescript of canon 497, § 3.

The third classification of religious edifices included in the scope of canon 497, § 3, is described by the very general phrase, *similis rationis aedes*. Canonists have provided little aid in the interpretation of this phrase, but it seems clear from the context and histor-

[9] Larraona, "Commentarium Codicis,"—*CpR*, V (1924), 431.

[10] Larraona, *loc. cit.*

ical background of the law that it refers to edifices in which the spiritual and corporal works of mercy and similar ministrations of piety and charity are carried out by the members of a religious institute.[11] Specifically, one may include in the term such institutions as hospitals and clinics, orphan asylums and homes for the poor, the aged and the delinquent.[12]

Article 2. Meaning of the Phrase *Separata a Domo*

There is a great diversity of opinion among canonists regarding the connotation of the phrase *separata a domo.* Some canonists consider the phrase as applying only to a material separation, while others believe that a formal separation, that is, a separation based on the nature of the work to be undertaken in the proposed edifice, is involved in a right interpretation of the phrase. Since a correct interpretation of the words *separata a domo* is the basis of a right understanding of the entire legislation of canon 497, § 3, it will be helpful to note the various opinions of the authors who treat the point, before any attempt will be made to draw any definite conclusions.

Fanfani[13] approaches the question from the viewpoint of material separation and states that a school, hospice or similar edifice is not separate from the religious house as long as it can be considered morally united to it. Beste's opinion is similar.[14] He holds that a building is separate from the religious house when it is not materially joined, that is, when it is either not under the same roof with the house, or not so contiguous to it that the house and edifice together form one group of buildings. Augustine[15] asserts that the phrase implies buildings which are distinct from the religious house to the extent that they are not under the same roof with the latter, but form a distinct and independent entity with respect to fire insurance, for example, or taxation.

[11] Cf. page 97.

[12] Beste, *Introductio in Codicem,* pp. 323-324; Fanfani, *De Iure Religiosorum,* n. 24.

[13] *De Iure Religiosorum,* n. 24.

[14] *Introductio in Codicem,* pp. 323-324.

[15] *Religious and Laymen,* p. 91.

According to the opinion of Claeys Bouuaert-Simenon, the factor of distance is not important to the concept of separation as understood by this canon.[16] An edifice is to be considered as separate from the religious house, according to this opinion, even if a very short distance intervenes, as long as it is truly separated. The point must be judged morally, with due regard being made for the original purpose of the religious house.

Coronata attempts to solve the question by resorting to a distinction between material and formal separation.[17] He states that an edifice is formally separated from the religious house if the work to be performed in it is not proper to the rule of the institute. Formal separation may exist, therefore, even when the edifice is materially joined to the religious house. Material separation is had, according to Coronata, when the edifice is opened or constructed at a considerable distance from the religious house.[18] He concludes that the special permission of canon 497, § 3, is necessary whenever an edifice is either formally or materially separated from the religious house.

Creusen [19] holds that there is question in this legislation of buildings which are constructed outside the property of the religious house, and are not constituted as independent communities. Oesterle [20] partly agrees with Creusen, stating that the special written permission of the local ordinary is required to establish a school, hospice or similar institute, if the building is to be opened or erected outside the limits of the property on which the religious house is located.

Larraona [21] approaches the interpretation of canon 497, § 3, from an entirely different angle than the previously mentioned authors. He emphasizes the element of filiality and is more concerned with pointing out the types of religious residences which cannot be established merely by this special written permission of the local

[16] Cf. *Manuale Iuris Canonici,* I (4. ed., Gandae et Leodii, 1934), n. 604.

[17] Cf. *Institutiones,* n. 524.

[18] Coronata estimates a considerable distance as being about 1,000 meters. Cf. *loc. cit.*

[19] "Fondation de Maisons Religieuses,"—*RCR,* XI (1935), 123.

[20] *Praelectiones Iuris Canonici,* I, 247.

[21] "Commentarium Codicis,"—*CpR,* V (1924), 432.

ordinary than he is preoccupied with determining which edifices are specifically included within the scope of the canon. The special permission of canon 497, § 3, is not sufficient, according to Larraona, unless there is question of opening or constructing a strictly filial house within the confines of the same city or, at least, of the same diocese as that in which the principal house to which it is attached is located. He adds that the term *aedes separata* is evidently used in this canon in contradistinction to *aedes non separata seu coniuncta* and, consequently, cannot be used correctly in reference to a house which is a great distance from a principal house. An edifice which is to be constructed or opened outside the diocese of the principal house should be simply called another religious house, Larraona asserts, and should be erected with the due formalities required by the law.[22]

This array of varying and often conflicting opinions indicates the difficulty involved in the interpretation of canon 497, § 3. However, an analysis of the principal elements of these various opinions, together with recourse to the general norm of canon 18 and to the context of the canon in question, may help to evolve a practical norm for application.

In accordance with the general principle of interpretation as stated in canon 18, ecclesiastical laws are to be understood according to the proper meaning of the words, considered in their text and context; if a doubt still remains, one is then to recur to parallel places in the Code, to the end and circumstances of the law and to the mind of the legislator. Applying this principle to canon 497, § 3, it seems quite apparent that the phrase *separata a domo* should be taken here in its proper sense as meaning materially distinct or disjoined from the religious house.

The distinction of a formal separation, that is, of a separation based on the nature and scope of the work to be performed in the proposed edifice, does not seem to be necessary or pertinent to a right interpretation of the phrase in question. If the scope of the work to be carried out in the new edifice is not proper to the rule of the institute, then certainly it cannot be said that the permission of the local ordinary is adequate authorization, in every case,

[22] *Loc. cit.*, note 385.

for the opening or erection of the building. To undertake work which is not proper to the rule of an institute is equivalent to making a change in the constitutions, and, in the case of an institute of pontifical right, this requires the permission of the Holy See by which the constitutions have been approved.[23] Moreover, even if one takes formal separation to mean simply that the new building is to be used for work which is different from that for which the principal religious house was established, but which is not outside the scope of the rule, the distinction seems equally unnecessary. Permission to erect a religious house implies the right to carry on all the works which are proper to the rule of an institute.[24] Consequently, the local ordinary must attach a specific contrary condition to his original authorization, if he wishes to exclude any of these works. Now, if the ordinary does make such a condition, the institute may not perform the works so restricted, even in an edifice attached to the religious house; if the ordinary does not impose any limitation, the religious may carry out *all* of their proper works in the religious house or in a building which is so joined to the religious house that it constitutes a material part of it.[25] There remains only one other situation for which to provide: the carrying out of the non-restricted works proper to the institute in an edifice which is not joined to the religious house.

In the opinion of the writer this latter is the case for which canon 497, § 3, intends to provide legislation. Consequently, any effort to interpret the phrase *separata a domo* must be based on some standard by which material separation can be judged to exist. It is not necessary, however, to accept material separation in a strict sense. The purpose of this law, which is to provide the local ordinary with a means of controlling the external activities of religious institutes within his diocese, is adequately served by accepting material separation in a broad sense as including that separation which is considered to exist according to the common judgment of men. It is the common doctrine among canonists that the existence of a moral union is sufficient in order that two buildings may be con-

[23] Can. 618, § 2, 1°.

[24] Can. 497, § 2.

[25] Can. 497, § 2, together with can. 497, § 3.

sidered in law as legally attached or joined to each other.[26] Hence, in a parallel sense, one may also speak of a moral separation. The material separation of which there is question in canon 497, § 3, may be interpreted, therefore, on the basis of a prudent moral judgment.

Coronata is apparently the only author who attempts to set a specific standard according to which an edifice may be considered materially separate (in a moral sense) from a principal religious house. He sets the distance of 1,000 meters as a criterion.[27] It does not appear, however, that this standard will always be satisfactory. In a populous city, for instance, where there is alien property between the religious house and the site of the proposed edifice, one certainly could not say that a moral union exists between the two institutions, even though a distance of much less than 1,000 meters separates them. In fact, the existence of a public thoroughfare between the religious house and the proposed building seems to exclude every judicial basis for considering a moral union to exist between them.[28] On the contrary, if the religious house were situated on a property comprising many acres of land, it would be possible for a building to be opened or constructed at a distance of more than 1,000 meters from the principal house and still be considered as morally joined to it.[29]

It seems evident, therefore, that any attempt to set a standard for judging material separation in terms of meters, yards, etc., will be unsatisfactory. In the opinion of the writer, the interpretation given by Creusen [30] and Oesterle [31] offers a sound and practical rule of application which is conformable both to the context of canon 497, § 3, and to the purpose of its legislation. According to this opinion the separation of which there is question here is verified only when the school, hospice or similar edifice is opened or con-

[26] Cf. Coronata, *Institutiones,* n. 524; Fanfani, *De Iure Religiosorum,* n. 24; Beste, *Introductio in Codicem,* 324; Claeys Bouuaert-Simenon, *Manuale Iuris Canonici,* I, n. 604.

[27] *Institutiones,* n. 524.

[28] Farrell, *The Local Ordinary and Women Religious of Pontifical Approval,* p. 70.

[29] Farrell, *loc. cit.*

[30] "Fondation de Maisons Religieuses,"—*RCR,* XI (1935), 123.

[31] *Praelectiones Iuris Canonici,* I, 247.

structed outside the limits of the property on which the principal religious house is located.

There is nothing in canon law which requires one to restrict the term religious house to a single building; a group of buildings or the whole property may be called materially the religious house.[32] In confirmation of this statement one may recur to several canons of the Code in which it is obvious that the legislator accepts the term *religious house* as embracing a complexus of buildings. Canon 514, § 1, for instance, gives to religious superiors of clerical institutes the right to administer Viaticum and Holy Communion to the professed religious, novices, guests and students, who reside day and night in their religious house. It is scarcely conceivable that all these various types of subjects would be lodged under the same roof; yet this canon considers all these persons as having a residence in the *religious house.* Likewise, canons 597, § 2, and 599, § 1, seem to indicate very clearly that a religious house, in the mind of the legislator, is not necessarily a single edifice or building.[33] Hence a moral union seems to exist between the various buildings on the religious property, so that all taken together could be said to constitute the religious house.

Moreover, since the permission to establish a religious house implies the right to undertake all of the proper works of the institute, unless the contrary be stated in the terms of the permission itself,[34] it seems logical to conclude that the religious also have the right to open or construct on their property the buildings necessary to carry out these works. The local ordinary is rightly presumed to realize this implication of the law, and hence there would be no

[32] Farrell, *loc. cit.*

[33] Cf. Oesterle, *loc. cit.*

Canon 597, § 2: Lege clausurae papalis afficitur tota domus quam communitas regularis inhabitat, cum hortis et viridariis accessui religiosorum reservatis; excluso, praeter publicum templum cum continente sacrario, etiam hospitio pro advenis, si adsit, et collocutorio, quod, quantum fieri potest, prope ianuam domus constitui debet.

Canon 599, § 1: Si domus regularium virorum adnexum habeat convictum pro alumnis internis vel alia opera religionis propria, separata saltem aedis pars, si fieri possit, religiosorum habitatio reservetur, clausurae legi subiecta.

[34] Can. 497, § 2.

question of prejudice to the rights which canon 497, § 3, intends to safeguard for him, if the religious institute proceeded to construct or open on its property the buildings which are needed to perform its proper works. On the other hand, the local ordinary cannot be expected to foresee an extension of activity which will take the religious outside the confines of their own property. It is for an extension of this kind, therefore, that canon 497, § 3, intends to provide by requiring a special written permission of the local ordinary.

However, as Larraona points out,[85] the separate edifice must be inhabited by a community which is truly filial in character; otherwise its erection must be conditioned on the full solemnities which the law requires. A house that is governed by a superior with *ex officio* power, even though this power be exercised vicariously in the name of the superior of a principal house, must be considered a religious house in the proper sense and subject to the formalities of canon 497, § 1, for its legitimate erection. In order to be truly filial, the edifice in question must be governed by the superior of the house to which it is attached, or by his simple delegate in the strict sense.[86]

On the assumption that the local ordinary has not imposed any contrary conditions regarding the proper works of an institute, one may draw the following conclusions pertinent to the legislation of canon 497, § 3:

(1) A special written permission of the local ordinary is necessary to open or construct an edifice which is outside the confines of the property on which the religious house (considered as a group of buildings) is located.

(2) This special permission is sufficient even though the religious house in question belongs to an exempt institute.

(3) The separate edifice must be strictly filial, being a residence which has no legal personality apart from that of the religious house to which it is attached.

[85] "Commentarium Codicis,"—*CpR,* V (1924), 432.

[86] The term "simple delegate" implies that the one who has charge of the edifice derives his power from a personal commission (*ex commissione a persona*) and not from an office (*ex munere*). Cf. Larraona, *loc. cit.;* Farrell, *The Local Ordinary and Women Religious of Pontifical Approval,* p. 71; also, page 31 of this work.

(4) No permission is necessary to open or construct a school, hospice or similar edifice within the confines of the property whereon the religious house is located, as long as the work which is there undertaken is proper to the rule of the institute and has not been restricted by a condition attached to the original permission to erect the house.

CHAPTER X

ALTERATION, TRANSFER AND RECOVERY OF A RELIGIOUS HOUSE

Canon 497, § 4: Ut constituta domus in alios usus convertatur, eaedem solemnitates requiruntur de quibus in § 1, nisi agatur de conversione quae, salvis fundationis legibus, ad internum regimen et disciplinam religiosam dumtaxat referatur.

ARTICLE 1. ALTERATION

THE alteration or conversion of a legitimately established religious house to other uses requires the observance of the same solemnities as are prescribed in canon 497, § 1, unless the change is of such a nature that, without prejudice to the laws of the charter of foundation, it affects only the internal order and the religious discipline of the house.

A religious house may be altered either materially or formally. Material changes are those which consist in enlarging, repairing or rebuilding an edifice; formal changes are those which affect the nature or purpose of the religious house. These latter may be either external or internal changes. A formal *external* change is one by which the house is converted to a use that will have external influence on the public, that is, on the faithful or the clergy of a diocese. A formal *internal* change, on the contrary, affects only the internal order of the religious institute and the juridic status or destination which the house has within the institute itself.[1]

In the concrete, an external change takes place when a school is changed into a public oratory, when a residence is made over into a college or retreat house, or when an apostolic school is converted into a school for extern students.[2] In each of these instances the

[1] Coronata, *Institutiones*, n. 525; Larraona, "Commentarium Codicis,"—*CpR*, V (1924), 436.

[2] Larraona, *loc. cit.*

change affects the external ministry of the religious house, that is, the works performed therein which concern the interests of the clergy or laity of the diocese. An internal conversion takes place when an ordinary house is raised to the dignity of a provincial or general house, when a residence is made over into a house of studies, or when an infirmary is converted into a library. In contrast to the above examples of external conversion, these changes pertain only to the internal order of the religious institute itself.

Canon 497, § 4, treats explicitly of both external and internal formal conversion. Before one proceeds to comment on the norms enunciated by this canon, however, it is necessary to emphasize the general principle that no change may be made in a legitimately established house, if this change runs counter to the articles contained in the charter of foundation or to the conditions imposed by the original authorization to erect the house.[3] Hence, if the religious house has been founded for a specific purpose through the generosity of a donor, his will must be respected. Any conversion that would involve a substantial change from the original intention of the donor would entail the obligation of obtaining both his consent and that of the local ordinary.[4] In fact, if the religious house was founded as the result of a last will and testament, the Sacred Congregation of the Council alone has the right to moderate or change the terms expressed in the charter of the foundation.[5] Even a conversion which does not exceed the limits of internal discipline would be forbidden, if it were contrary to the stipulations or articles of the foundation charter.

Moreover, it has been pointed out in the commentary on canon 497, § 2, that the local ordinary has the right to attach conditions, conformable to the common law, to his permission to establish a religious house. Frequently, too, a contract is drawn up between the local ordinary and the religious superiors at the time when a new religious house is being established. The terms of this contract as

[3] Cf. can. 497, §§ 2 and 4.

[4] Cf. cans. 497, § 4; 1515, §§1-2; 1516, § 2. Cf. also Farrell, *The Local Ordinary and Women Religious of Pontifical Approval*, p. 63, note 34 a.

[5] Can. 1517. Cf. also Augustine, *Religious and Laymen*, p. 94.

well as any legitimate conditions imposed by the local ordinary in the granting of his authorization must be respected.[6]

Prescinding from the obligations arising from the articles in the charter of foundation and from the contract or conditions imposed by the local ordinary, one may point out as applicable the following norms for the conversion of a religious house:

(1) Materially, the building may be enlarged, repaired or rebuilt, for such changes do not affect the legal status of the religious house as a moral person. In some cases, however, the laws pertinent to the alienation of temporal goods and to the contraction of debts will be involved in a material conversion and therefore must be observed.[7]

(2) A formal internal conversion, that is, one which pertains solely to the internal order and religious discipline of the institute, may be made without the consent of the Holy See or of the local ordinary. There is only one exception to this general rule: the conversion of a house into a novitiate, when the institute is of pontifical right, requires the permission of the Holy See.[8]

(3) A formal *external* change, which cannot be considered as included either implicitly or explicitly in the original permission of the local ordinary, is equivalent to a new foundation and requires the observance of the complete formalities of a canonical erection.[9] It must be noted, however, that it is possible for even formal external changes to be included, at least implicitly, in the original permission to erect the religious house. It has been previously demonstrated in the course of this work that the right to carry out any and all of the proper works of an institute is included in the general con-

[6] It must be remembered, however, that if the local ordinary has granted an unrestricted permission for the erection of the religious house, the religious obtain an acquired right to the performance of all the works which are proper to their rule. The local ordinary cannot change the terms of his authorization at a later date and impose new restrictions. Cf. page 94 of this work; also Larraona, "Commentarium Codicis,"—*CpR,* V (1924), 430.

[7] Cans. 534, § 1; 535; 1530 sqq.

[8] Can. 554.

[9] Coronata, *Institutiones,* n. 525; Schaefer, *De Religiosis,* n. 87, p. 138; Farrell, *The Local Ordinary and Women Religious of Pontifical Approval,* p. 64.

cession of permission to establish a religious house.[10] Consequently, unless the admission of the religious to the diocese, or the permission for the establishment of their house, restricted the institute to a particular part of its work, the law considers all the works proper to the rule of the institute as being included in the permission to erect the house. In other words, a correct interpretation of canon 497, § 4, demands that its norm be related to canon 497, § 2, and that only those conversions, even external ones, which exceed the limits of the original permission to establish the religious house, are to be considered as equivalent to the erection of a new house.[11]

It is readily apparent, therefore, that one cannot insist too strongly upon the importance of drawing up a written contract or agreement which specifies the purpose or purposes for which the religious house is to be destined, on the occasion of its establishment. It will be to the advantage of both the local ordinary and the religious superiors to determine these matters beforehand in order to avoid misunderstandings later on.[12]

(4) Formal conversions which are at the same time internal and external require the observance of the solemnities of canon 497, § 1. The text of section 4 of this canon clearly indicates that a change may be permitted, without recourse to the local ordinary or to the Holy See, *only* when it pertains to the internal order or discipline of the institute. Therefore, the conversion of a house into a school which is to be open to extern students as well as to candidates for the religious institute would require the formalities of a canonical erection as prescribed by canon 497, § 1.[13]

[10] Cf. page 93, see also can. 497, § 2.

[11] Larraona, "Commentarium Codicis,"—*CpR,* V (1924), 434-435; Fanfani, *De Iure Religiosorum,* n. 25; Wernz-Vidal, *De Religiosis,* n. 71; Farrell, *The Local Ordinary and Women Religious of Pontifical Approval,* p. 64.

[12] The Fathers of the II Council of Baltimore urged such a pact.—*Acta et Decreta Concilii Plenarii Baltimorensis II (1866),* (Baltimorae, 1894), n. 203.

[13] When a house is converted into an apostolic school, destined only for the training of boys who are in a wide sense postulants of the institute, the nature of the change, that is, whether it is external or merely internal, is not entirely clear. Vermeersch-Creusen (*Epitome,* I, n. 560) and Schaefer (*De Religiosis,* n. 87, p. 138) assert that it is an external change requiring the observance of the norm of canon 497, § 1. This opinion is based on the contention that the local ordinary may be averse to having an apostolic school in a particular

Article 2. Transfer

The Code does not expressly legislate for the case of transferring a religious house from the place where it has been canonically established to another location. The question has practical value, however, since circumstances may often occur in which religious will desire or be compelled to transfer the location of their house. Canonists discuss the point, but do not agree in determining how far a religious house may be moved before the transfer must be considered equivalent to a new foundation.

However, it is certain that in many specific instances any transfer from the original site will be forbidden or at least definitely restricted. The articles in the charter of foundation and the original permission to establish a religious house must be carefully examined in order to determine whether any conditions regarding the matter of transfer have been stipulated, for it is certain that no transfer may be made which exceeds the limits of any restrictions, either explicit or implicit, which are stated in the permission for the canonical erection, or imposed by the will of the founders or donors.[14]

Moreover, if the religious house has a church or public oratory

place. Coronata (*Institutiones*, n. 525, p. 638, note 5) and Larraona ("Commentarium Codicis,"—*CpR*, V [1924], 436, note 402) take the opposite view. Larraona states that the establishment of an apostolic school is a work pertinent to the internal order of a religious institute, while Coronata holds that the contention of the other opinion cannot be proved, and that custom, which is the best interpreter of law, neither before nor after the Code has required any special permission for the establishment of one of these schools in a religious house. In the opinion of the writer, the argument of Coronata, together with the fact, as alleged by Larraona, that the training of candidates is a work which is not only proper to every institute, but necessary to its continuance in existence, render this latter interpretation the more sound and probable opinion. It must be repeated, however, that the opening of an apostolic school, as well as any other kind of school, is, under the circumstances discussed on page 97 of this work, subject to the norm of canon 497, § 3.

[14] Larraona, "Commentarium Codicis,"—*CpR*, V (1924), 419; Farrell, *The Local Ordinary and Women Religious of Pontifical Approval*, p. 65. It may be noted that an implicit restriction of transfer would exist if the local ordinary approved the erection of the religious house in connection with a definite parish or on a fixed and determinate site.

attached to it, another factor must be taken into consideration: the special permission of the local ordinary which is required for the erection of a church or public oratory involves the approval by him of the site of the sacred edifice.[15] It is evident that this factor can be so restrictive that it will prevent almost any change in the site of the religious house itself.[16]

Finally, a religious house cannot be transferred outside the limits of the diocese in which it has been canonically erected. The consent given by a local ordinary is valid only for the establishment of a religious house within the territory of his proper jurisdiction.

Outside of these instances of direct or, at least, indirect restriction of the site, the question of transferring a religious house remains a subject of controversy. Most of the canonists agree that if the religious house is moved to a location outside of the municipality where it was originally established, a new act of canonical erection is necessary.[17] There is no such unanimity of opinion, however, concerning the question of transfer from one location to another within the confines of the same city, town or village.

The more common opinion holds that a religious house may be moved anywhere within the limits of a municipality without the permission of the local ordinary or of the Holy See.[18] Fanfani however holds that if a religious house is moved a distance of two or three miles, even within the same city, such an act appears to be equivalent to a new foundation.[19] Schaefer is even more strict in his interpretation, contending that a transfer from one site to another within the same city or town requires the permission of the local ordinary.[20]

In the old law the question of the transfer of a religious house

15 Can. 1162, § 4.

16 Farrell, *The Local Ordinary and Women Religious of Pontifical Approval*, p. 66.

17 Larraona, "Commentarium Codicis,"—*CpR*, V (1924), 419; Fanfani, *De Iure Religiosorum*, n. 23; Schaefer, *De Religiosis*, n. 87, p. 139; Gerster, *Ius Religiosorum in Compendium Redactum*, p. 29.

18 Gerster, *loc. cit.;* Larraona, *loc. cit.;* Augustine, *Religious and Laymen*, p. 93; Coronata, *Institutiones*, n. 525.

19 *Loc. cit.*

20 *Loc. cit.*

was expressly treated. Leo XIII, in his Constitution "*Romanos Pontifices,*" decreed that a monastery could not be moved from one place to another without the permission of the Holy See and of the local ordinary.[21] Pope Leo based his legislation upon an earlier decree of Boniface VIII, which he cited as legal precedent for his prohibition.[22]

In both the decree of Boniface VIII and the constitution of Leo XIII the term *locus* was used in referring to the transfer of a monastery from one site to another. Most pre-Code canonists interpreted this word in the sense of a municipality, and consequently concluded that a transfer was forbidden by law only when the move involved a change from one city, town or village to another.[23]

Larraona [24] asserts that this doctrine stands confirmed both before and after the Code by the practice of the Roman Curia in approving the transfer of religious houses from one part of the Eternal City to another without the permission of ecclesiastical authority. In further support of his opinion Larraona puts forth the argument that in preliminary editions of the Code the text of canon 497, § 1, required the formalities of a canonical erection both for the erection and the transfer of a religious house.[25] He concludes that the omission of the words regarding the transfer, in the approved edition of the Code, evidences the mind of the legislator not to impose the formalities of a canonical erection in the case of the transfer of a religious house from one place to another.

These arguments as presented by Larraona, together with the added force of canon, 6, 4°, which declares that when a doubt exists

[21] Leo XIII, const. "*Romanos Pontifices,*" 8 maii 1881, § 22: ". . . dimovere de *loco* instituta alioque transferre [nequeunt]. . . ."—*Fontes*, n. 582.

[22] This decree forbade religious "ad habitandum domos vel loca quaecumque de novo recipere, seu hactenus recepta mutare. . . ."—C. 1, *de excessibus Praelatorum,* V, 6, in VI°.

[23] Pignatelli, *Consultationes Canonicae,* tom. X, consult. 74, n. 3; Pichler, *Epitome Iuris Canonici,* lib. V, tit. 33, n. 29; Bouix, *De Iure Regularium,* tom. I, pars II, sect. 2, cap. 2, § 3; Vermeersch, *De Religiosis Institutis et Personis,* I (2. ed., Bruges, 1907), n. 115; Wernz, *Ius Decretalium,* III, n. 168; Piatus Montensis, *Praelectiones Iuris Regularis,* II, 279, notes 7 and 8.

[24] "Commentarium Codicis,"—*CpR,* V (1924), 420.

[25] "Ad erigendam *vel transferendam* domum religiosam . . . " were the words of the 1914 edition; Larraona, *ibid.,* note 341.

concerning the discrepancy of a canon from the old law one is not to depart from the import of the former legislation, give a sound juridical basis for this opinion, based on pre-Code doctrinal interpretation, according to which the solemnities of a canonical erection are not required for the transfer of a religious house from one site to another within the same municipality. As noted previously, however, this conclusion must be understood as being qualified by possible restrictions from another source, such as the articles in the charter of foundation or the terms of the original authorization for the erection of the religious house.

Granted, therefore, that the transfer of a religious house within the limits of a town, city or village is not equivalent to the new erection of a religious house, does this mean that the move can be made without any permission whatsoever? It seems that it cannot. Rather it appears that the permission of the local ordinary will be necessary in nearly every case.

In the first place, there is usually at least an implicit restriction on the location of a religious house in every authorization for its canonical erection. The local ordinary does not simply approve the establishment of a religious house; rather, he authorizes a house to be established in connection with a certain parish, school, hospital, etc., or he permits a house to be erected on a site which has been determined beforehand by agreement with the religious superiors. Thus, even though the local ordinary does not expressly state, in granting the requisite permission for the erection of the religious house, that he forbids it to be moved, nevertheless this implicit restriction seems to suffice for preventing any change from the approved location without a new act of consent.[26]

Moreover, even in the hypothesis that the permission of the local ordinary for the establishment of a religious house contained no implicit restriction concerning the location of the edifice, the purpose of the legislation on the canonical erection of religious houses

[26] Larraona ("Commentarium Codicis,"—*CpR,* V [1924], 419) also seems to admit this same conclusion: ". . . *ex se* et *ratione domus* venia non requiritur neque S. Sedis neque Ordinarii loci ad hanc translationem intra eandem civitatem eundemve locum complendam. . . . Diximus *ex se,* quia aliud dicendum esset si licentia ad erectionem concessa ita fuit sub hoc respectu limitata ut explicite vel implicite, sed clare certoque, translationem excluderet."

seems to require the ordinary's permission for a transfer to another part of the city. The Code demands the consent of the local ordinary for the erection of a religious house precisely because it wishes to give him the right to judge the opportuneness of the proposed foundation in relation to the place where it is to be made. This fact is evident from the history of the legislation in this matter. Now, it is clear that this opportuneness may vary from place to place within the same city; in fact, it will certainly vary in a large city where there are many religious houses.

Finally, an argument from analogy may be drawn from canon 497, § 3. If a special written permission of the local ordinary is necessary for the opening or the construction of a school, a hospice or any similar edifice, separate from the religious house, it is logical to conclude that the local ordinary's permission will be equally required for the transfer of the house itself to a site which is outside the confines of the property on which it was originally established. It appears, then, that the only permissible transfer without the consent of the local ordinary is the one which is made within the limits of the property whereon the religious house has been canonically erected.

Article 3. Recovery of a Religious House

The dispersion of religious communities by reason of the devastation of war and the persecution of civil governments presents a practical problem concerning the status of the religious house from which a community has been expelled. In discussing this point one may also consider the case of a religious house which has been voluntarily abandoned, since the principals involved are similar.

The point at issue is: may the religious recover an abandoned house without being obliged to resort to a new act of canonical erection? Canon 102, § 1, states that a moral person is by nature perpetual and can become extinct only by legal suppression under competent ecclesiastical authority, or by its failure to be operative for a period of one hundred years. Hence, it is clear that if a religious house is legitimately suppressed, on the occasion of its abandonment, an attempt to re-establish it on the same location will require a new act of canonical erection. Certain difficulties arise, however, when one endeavors to apply the other legitimate means of extinguishing a moral person to the case of an abandoned religious house, namely, its failure to be operative for a period of one hundred years. Specifically, one may ask: Will a religious house lose its juridical status if the religious *voluntarily* desert it for a period of less than one hundred years? And, on the other hand, will a forceful and violent expulsion from the religious house juridically effect its extinction even though it extend for a period beyond one hundred years?

Pre-Code canonists discussed the question of the status of an abandoned religious house primarily on the basis of whether the community had left the house voluntarily or whether it had been expelled by force. The time element, that is, the number of years during which the religious house was not used, received only secondary consideration.[27]

The common opinion of these pre-code canonists can be stated in the form of a distinction: if the religious voluntarily left their house, either licitly or illicitly, the solemnities of a canonical erection were necessary if canonical residence was to be resumed; if the abandonment had been caused by external force, the religious house retained its legal status.[28] The second member of the distinction was qualified, however, by two exceptions: if the Holy See had ordered or confirmed the alienation of the temporal goods of the exiled community, or if the religious had been away from the house for such a long time that they could be morally considered to have renounced their right to the abandoned house, the formalities of a canonical erection were held necessary if a re-establishment of the house was to be effected.[29]

Most of the modern canonists adopt the same distinction between forceful and voluntary abandonment of a religious house, in their

[27] The absence of footnotes to canon 102, § 1, in all probability indicates that this is a new law. Hence, the reason for the failure of the older canonists to include the time factor in their discussion is readily apparent.

[28] Ferraris, *Bibliotheca*, s. v. "conventus," art. I, n. 8; Wernz, *Ius Decretalium*, III, n. 618; Bouix, *De Iure Regularium*, tom. I, pars III, sect. 2, cap. 1-3; Appeltern, *Compendium Praelectionum Iuris Regularis*, q. 658, p. 592; Vermeersch, *De Religiosis Institutis et Personis*, I, n. 122.

[29] Cf. Bouix, *loc. cit.*; Wernz, *loc. cit.*; Vermeersch, *loc. cit.*

solution of the question of recovery. They do not agree, however, in the conclusions which they draw from the distinction.

In the case of a voluntary desertion, Balmes,[30] Mothon [31] and Fanfani [32] make no reference to the length of time during which the religious are absent from their house, but simply state that, if the community freely departs from the religious house, the formalities of a canonical erection must be repeated if legal residence is to be resumed.

Pejška [33] and Coronata [34] state that in the case of a spontaneous desertion the religious may return anytime within the period of one hundred years without being obliged to renew the formalities of a canonical erection. Goyeneche [35] also supports this view and adds that a canonical erection grants the right of existence as a religious house not solely to the various individual religious who are sent to the particular house by the legitimate superiors, but to all the members of the entire religious institute. Hence, even if all the original members of the religious house die during the period of absence, the rights consequent upon the canonical erection remain firm.

The opinion of these last named canonists must be held as the one which is more conformable to the law of the Code. Canon 102, § 1, states clearly and without qualification that a moral person does not lose its juridical status until it has ceased to be operative for a period of one hundred years. Consequently, on the basis of this canon, it is clear that even a voluntary desertion of a religious house, as long as it is not prolonged beyond one hundred years, does not extinguish the legal rights which derived their original existence from the canonical erection of the house.

The opinion of canonists is equally divided with regard to the question of recovery when the religious have been forcefully driven

[30] *Les Religieux à Voeux Simples d'après le Code* (Paray-le-Monial, 1921), 42, note 1.

[31] *Traité sur L'État Religieux,* art. 105, p. 134.

[32] *De Iure Religiosorum,* n. 24.

[33] *Ius Canonicum Religiosorum,* p. 56.

[34] *Institutiones,* n. 525, p. 638, note 1.

[35] "Consultationes,"—*CpR,* VII (1926), 394-396.

from their house. Schaefer [36] and Mothon [37] hold that a religious house ceases to have legal existence after one hundred years, no matter what may have been the cause of its abandonment. They argue that, since canon 102, § 1, makes no distinction, the cause of departure is immaterial. On the other hand, Coronata [38] asserts that expulsion by force cannot effect a loss of juridic rights. He bases his contention on the principle, enunciated in canon 103, § 1, that an act performed either by a physical or moral person under extrinsic violence which cannot be resisted has no juridical value and may be considered as non-existent. The norm of canon 102, § 1, Coronata adds, must be understood as applying only to a voluntary desertion of a religious house.[39] Hence, a religious house never ceases to exist legally if it has been abandoned by reason of external force.

Fanfani [40] and Pejška [41] support this view of Coronata with certain qualifications. The former remarks that the Holy See may dispose otherwise, or that the permission for the erection of the religious house may contain conditions, relative to possible future dispersion, which, if verified, will effect a loss of juridic status. In this latter eventuality, according to Fanfani, the religious lose their right to recover the house, not by reason of the expulsion, but on the occasion of it and by virtue of the fulfillment of a condition imposed by competent ecclesiastical authority. Pejška accepts the norm which was held by pre-Code authors who stated that the religious may be presumed to have tacitly renounced their right to their house, if a very long time has elapsed between the date of their expulsion from the house and their subsequent attempt to recover it. He states that this tacit renunciation severs the bond between subject and object, which is the basis of every right, and thus brings it about that the right to recover the house may be morally considered to be pre-empted. However, this opinion seems hardly tenable in view of the fact, already demonstrated, that a religious house retains its moral person-

[36] *De Religiosis,* n. 88, p. 141.

[37] *Traité sur L'État Religieux,* art. 105, p. 134.

[38] *Institutiones,* n. 525, p. 638, note 1.

[39] *Loc. cit.*

[40] *De Iure Religiosorum,* nn. 24, 520.

[41] *Ius Canonicum Religiosorum,* p. 56.

ality until it has been legitimately suppressed or has failed to be operative for a period of one hundred years.

It appears that one may arrive at a sound juridical conclusion in this matter of determining the legal status of a religious house which has been forcefully abandoned, by drawing upon the opinions of both Coronata and Fanfani. Since canon 103, § 1, clearly states that any act which is done by a moral person because of irresistible external force is considered in law as non-existent, the forceful abandonment of a religious house cannot be deemed in strict law as having any effect upon the legal status of that house. However, other factors may intervene during the period of absence, or on the occasion of it, to effect a change in the juridical status of the religious house so as to make recovery impossible without recourse to a new act of canonical erection.

In the first place, as Fanfani points out,[42] the authorization for the erection of a religious house may impose conditions which, even in the event of forceful expulsion, will effect a loss of juridic rights. Also, legitimate suppression may have been decreed by competent ecclesiastical authority, and, under certain circumstances, prescription, according to the norms of law, may deprive the religious of their legal right. In the matter of prescription, however, it must be kept in mind that the loss of the material edifice is not always equivalent to a loss of moral personality for the religious house. The legal title of prescription can effect the extinction of a moral personality only if, by reason of a previous contract or condition, the religious house has been restricted to a definite and fixed site.

In conclusion, it is apparent that the theoretical right of a religious community to recover an abandoned house cannot be applied in every particular case because of the circumstances of fact which are often present to nullify this right.[43]

Closely related to the question of the recovery of an abandoned religious house is the question concerning the provision which can or should be made for a community which has been expelled from its canonically established house. This question arises when a dispersed community is able to resume the practice of the common life upon

[42] *Loc. cit.*

[43] Goyeneche, "Consultationes,"—*CpR,* VII (1926), 395.

repairing to another country or diocese. The solution of this problem, as is evident from the discussion in the paragraphs immediately preceding, will depend upon the legal condition of the house from which the religious have departed. As long as this house retains its canonical status, the law considers it to be the legitimate residence of the exiled community. Consequently, these religious do not need to be canonically established in the place to which they have fled; rather, it seems that they need only the permission of the local ordinary to stay in his diocese and that the works to be performed by them during their sojourn can be arranged by mutual agreement between the religious superior and the local ordinary.[44]

On the contrary, if the abandoned religious house has lost its juridic standing on the occasion of the expulsion or during the absence of the community, provision must be made for the canonical erection of a house in another place. This situation is equivalent to making a new foundation, and hence the complete formalities required by law must be observed.

Thus far the discussion concerning the provision to be made for an exiled community has been restricted to the question of law. As for the question of fact, Mothon[45] summarizes the various procedures which were adopted by local ordinaries in England, Belgium, Italy, Spain and Holland, when communities exiled from France fled to their jurisdiction. Four different systems were adopted by these bishops:

(1) The majority authorized residence or sojourn in their dioceses without resorting to a new act of canonical erection.[46]

(2) Others, together with the permission for the sojourn of the religious, proceeded to grant a new canonical foundation by virtue of their ordinary power.

[44] Mothon (*Traité sur L'État Religieux,* art. 91, p. 123) believes that a local ordinary may grant permission for a canonical erection effective only for the time the community remains in his diocese. However, since the moral personality of the religious house from which the community has been dispersed continues to exist, such a procedure hardly seems justifiable and is certainly not necessary.

[45] *Loc. cit.*

[46] On the basis of the principles enunciated above, this must be held to have been the best juridical solution.

(3) Still others recurred to the Holy See, which accorded the canonical erection or transfer in accordance with the petition of the bishop.

(4) Communities which belonged to congregations were content with the permission of temporary sojourn granted by the bishop, and, without bothering to obtain consent for a canonical establishment, placed themselves under the authority of a vicar of their general or provincial superior.

CONCLUSIONS

1. A religious house, in the strict canonical sense, is a permanent and legitimately established foundation, where the religious practice the common life, in accordance with the constitutions of their institute and under the direction of their proper superiors.

2. The complete formalities of canonical erection are necessary only for a religious house in this strict sense. Villas, hospices, farmhouses and other residences, which are used for purely secular purposes by a religious institute, are not subject to the norms of canonical erection.

3. A special written permission of the local ordinary is needed, but it also suffices, for the opening or construction of dependent edifices, such as a school, hospital, orphanage, etc., which are separate from the legitimately established house of which they are a part, that is, located outside the property whereon the religious house is situated.

4. This special written permission of the local ordinary also suffices as a requisite for the erection of strictly filial houses, that is, of houses which have no legal existence or moral personality apart from the independent religious house to which they are attached.

5. A formal decree of canonical erection, issued by the competent religious superior, is not necessary for the validity of a new foundation. It is sufficient that the superior acknowledge the foundation as a religious house of his institute, for, once the requisite authorization has been given, the religious house becomes an ecclesiastical moral person by the prescript of the law itself.

6. It cannot be proved that the required permission of the local ordinary must be given in writing in order to be valid. Rather, this solemnity seems to be prescribed by the Code as a directive norm, in order that the legal status of the religious house may be vindicated in the external forum by means of a written document.

7. The vicar general and the vicar capitular are generally competent to authorize the erection of a religious house. Consequently these dignitaries may permit a religious institute to erect a house,

unless their faculties are restricted in a particular case, by principles stated elsewhere in the Code, or, in the case of the vicar general, by special reservation of the bishop.

8. A diocesan institute needs the permission of the ordinary of the diocese wherein its motherhouse is located only for the first foundation in another diocese. Once the institute has been extended to another diocese, there is required only the permission of the ordinary of that diocese when subsequent foundations are to be authorized.

9. The erection of a monastery by nuns who by special prescript of the Holy See are professed with only simple vows requires the approbation of the Holy See and of the local ordinary.

10. In granting permission for the erection of a religious house, the local ordinary may attach conditions, which are in conformity to the common law, by virtue of which the religious in this particular house are restricted in the performance of their proper works. However, these conditions must be attached to the permission itself, or they will have no binding force before the law.

11. The transfer of a religious house outside the confines of the town or city in which it has been canonically erected is equivalent to a new foundation and requires the observance of the same solemnities as for the erection of a new house.

12. Without the consent of the local ordinary a religious house may not be moved outside the limits of the property whereon it has been canonically established.

13. A religious house which has been voluntarily abandoned by a community does not lose its legal status until it has been legitimately suppressed or has ceased to function as a religious house for more than one hundred years.

14. A religious house from which the community has been forcefully expelled can retain its juridical status and the rights consequent to it, even though the period of exile may extend beyond one hundred years.

BIBLIOGRAPHY

Sources

Acta Apostolicae Sedis, Commentarium Officiale, Romae, 1909—

Acta et Decreta Concilii Plenarii Americae Latinae, Romae, 1902.

Acta et Decreta Concilii Plenarii Baltimorensis II (1866), Baltimorae, 1894.

Acta et Decreta Concilii Plenarii Baltimorensis III (1884), Baltimorae, 1886.

Acta et Decreta Sacrorum Conciliorum Recentiorum, Collectio Lacensis, 7 vols., Friburgi Brisgoviae, 1870-1890.

Acta Sanctae Sedis, 41 vols., Romae, 1865-1908.

Bullarum Diplomatum et Privilegiorum Sanctorum Romanorum Pontificum Taurinensis Editio, 25 vols., Augustae Taurinorum, 1857-1872.

Canones et Decreta Sacrosanctae Oecumenici Concilii Tridentini, Taurini, 1913.

Codex Iuris Canonici Pii X Pontificis Maximi iussu digestus Benedicti Papae XV auctoritate promulgatus, Romae: Typis Polyglottis Vaticanis, 1917.

Codicis Iuris Canonici Fontes cura Emi. Petri Card. Gasparri editi, 9 vols., Romae [postea Civitate Vaticana]: Typis Polyglottis Vaticanis, 1923-1939. (Vols. VII-IX *ed. cura et studio Emi. Iustiniani Card. Serédi.*)

Collectanea in usum Secretariae Sacrae Congregationis Episcoporum et Regularium, ed. Bizzarri, Romae, 1885.

Collectanea S. Congregationis de Propaganda Fide, 2 vols., Romae: Typographia Polyglotta S. C. de Propaganda Fide, 1907.

Corpus Iuris Canonici, editio Lipsiensis secunda, post Aemilii Richteri curas—instruxit Aemilius Freidberg, 2 vols., Lipsiae, 1879-1881.

Corpus Iuris Civilis, Vol. III, *Novellae Constitutiones,* ed. R. Schoell. Opus Schoelli morte interceptum absolvit G. Kroll, Berolini apud Weidmannos, 1928-1929.

Decisiones Sacrae Romanae Rotae coram Ratto, Romae, 1752.

Decreta Authentica Congregationis Sacrorum Rituum, 6 vols., Romae, 1898-1927.

Mansi, Joannes, *Sacrorum Conciliorum Nova et Amplissima Collectio,* 53 vols. in 60, Parisiis, Arnhem, Lipsiae, 1901-1927.

Normae secundum quas S. Cong. Ep. et Reg. procedere solet in approbandis Novis Institutis Votorum Simplicium, Typis S. Cong. de Propaganda Fide, 1901.

Pallotini, S., *Collectio Omnium Conciliorum et Resolutionum quae in causis propositis apud Sacram Congregationem Cardinalium S. Concilii Tridentini Interpretum prodierunt ab eius institutione anno MDLXIV ad annum MDCCCLX, distinctis titulis alphabetico ordine per materias digesta,* 18 vols., Romae, 1868-1893.

Sacrae Romanae Rotae Decisiones Recentiores, 19 partes in 25 vols., Romae, 1623-1703.

Authors

Alteserra, F., *Opera Omnia*, tom. III, *Asceticon sive Originum Rei Monasticae*, Neapoli, 1777.

Appeltern, Vcitor, *Compendium Praelectionum Iuris Regularis Adm. R. P. Piati Montani ad Recentissimas Leges Ecclesiasticas Redactum*, 2. ed., Parisiis, 1913.

[Bachofen], Charles Augustine, *A Commentary on the New Code of Canon Law*, 8 vols., Vol. III, *Religious and Laymen*, 5. ed., St. Louis, Herder, 1938.

Bakalarczyk, Richardus, *De Novitiatu*, The Catholic University of America Canon Law Studies, n. 36, Washington, D. C.: The Catholic University of America, 1927.

Balmes, Hilaire, *Les Religieux à Voeux Simples d'après le Code*, Paray-le-Monial, 1921.

Barbosa, Augustinus, *Collectanea Doctorum in Varia Concilii Tridentini Decreta et Canones*, Lugduni, 1657.

Bastien, Pierre, *Directoire Canonique à L'usage des Congrégations à Voeux Simples*, 6. ed., Paris, 1923.

Benedictus XIV, *De Synodo Diocesana*, 3 vols., Romae, 1788.

Berutti, Chr., *Institutiones Iuris Canonici*, Vol. III, Taurini: Marietti, 1936.

Beste, Udalricus, *Introductio in Codicem*, St. John's Abbey: Collegeville, Minn., 1938.

Blat, Albertus, *Commentarium Textus Codicis Iuris Canonici*, 6 vols., Vol. II, *Ius de Religiosis et Laicis iuxta Codicis Ordinem*, Romae, 1921.

Bonal, A., *Institutiones Canonicae*, 2 vols., Parisiis, Lugduni, 1898.

Bondini, Aloisius, *De Privilegio Exemptionis seu de Regularium Immunitate ab Ordinariorum Locorum Iurisdictione prout in Novo Iuris Canonici Codice Sancitur*, Romae, 1919.

Bouix, Dominicus, *Tractatus de Iure Regularium*, 3. ed., 2 vols., Parisiis, 1882.

Bouscaren, T. L., *Canon Law Digest*, 3 vols., Milwaukee: Bruce, 1934-1941.

Cajetanus, Felix, *Iuris Canonici Universi Commentarius*, 3 vols., Monachii, 1705.

Campagna, Angelo, *Il Vicario Generale del Vescovo*, The Catholic University of America Canon Law Studies, n. 66, Washington, D. C.: The Catholic University of America, 1931.

Catholic Encyclopedia, The, 15 vols., New York, 1907-1912.

Chelodi, Ioannes, *Ius de Personis Iuxta Codicem Iuris Canonici*, 2. ed., Tridenti: Libr. Tridentum, 1927.

Claeys-Bouuaert, F.-Simenon, G., *Manuale Iuris Canonici ad usum Seminariorum*, 3 vols., Gandae et Leodii, Vols. I and III, 4. ed., 1934; Vol. II, 2. ed., 1935.

Connolly, Nicholas, *The Canonical Erection of Parishes*, The Catholic University of America Canon Law Studies, n. 114, Washington, D. C.: The Catholic University, 1938.

Coronata, Matthaeus Conte a, *Institutiones Iuris Canonici ad usum Utriusque Cleri et Scholarum*, 5 vols., Vols. I-II, 2. ed., Taurini: Marietti, 1939.

Creusen, Joseph-Garesché, Edw.-Ellis, Adam, *Religious Men and Women in the Code,* 3. English ed., Milwaukee: Bruce, 1940.

De Luca, Ioannes Baptista, *Il Dottore Volgare,* 15 vols., Romae, 1673-1693.

De Meester, Alphonsus, *Juris Canonici et Juris Canonico-Civilis Compendium,* nova editio, 3 vols. in 4, Bruges, 1921-1928.

Devoti, Ioannes, *Institutionum Canonicarum Libri IV,* 2 vols., Leodii, 1860.

Donatus, Hyacinthus, *Rerum Regularium Praxis Resolutoria,* 4 vols., Neapoli, 1652.

Engel, Ludovicus, *Collegium Universum Iuris Canonici,* Venetiis, 1750.

Fagnanus, Prosperus, *Commentarium in Librum Decretalium,* 3 vols., Venetiis, 1709.

Fanfani, Ludovicus, *De Iure Religiosorum ad Normam Codicis Iuris Canonici,* 2. ed., Taurini: Marietti, 1925.

Farrell, Benjamin, *The Rights and Duties of the Local Ordinary Regarding Congregations of Women Religious of Pontifical Approval,* The Catholic University of America Canon Law Studies, n. 128, Washington, D. C.: The Catholic University of America Press, 1941.

Ferraris, F. Lucius, *Prompta Bibliotheca Canonica, Iuridica, Moralis, Theologica, necnon Ascetica, Polemica, Rubricistica, Historica,* 9 vols., Romae, 1885-1899.

Gerster, Thomas Villanova a Zeil, *Ius Religiosorum in Compendium Redactum,* Taurini: Marietti, 1935.

Geser, Fintan, *The Canon Law Governing Communities of Sisters,* St. Louis: Herder, 1938.

Goodwine, John, *The Right of the Church to Acquire Temporal Goods,* The Catholic University of America Canon Law Studies, n. 131, Washington, D. C.: The Catholic University of America Press, 1941.

Grandclaude, E., *Ius Canonicum iuxta Ordinem Decretalium,* 3 vols., Parisiis, 1882.

Melo, Antonius, *De Exemptione Regularium,* The Catholic University of America Canon Law Studies, n. 12, Washington, D. C.: The Catholic University of America, 1921.

Migne, Jacques Paul, *Patrologiae Cursus Completus, Series Latina,* 221 vols., Parisiis, 1844-1864.

Molitor, Raphael, *Religiosi Iuris Capita Selecta,* Ratisbonae, 1909.

Monacelli, Franciscus, *Formularium Legale Practicum Fori Ecclesiastici,* 4 vols., Romae, 1713.

Mothon, Joseph Pie, *Traité sur L'État Religieux,* Paris, 1922.

Oesterle, Gerardus, *Praelectiones Iuris Canonici,* Vol. I, Romae, 1931.

Orth, Clement, *The Approbation of Religious Institutes,* The Catholic University of America Canon Law Studies, n. 71, Washington, D. C.: The Catholic University of America, 1931.

Pejška, Joseph, *Ius Canonicum Religiosorum,* 3. ed., Friburgi Brisgoviae: Herder, 1927.

Petra, Vincentius, *Commentaria ad Constitutiones Apostolicas,* 5 vols. in 2, Venetiis, 1729.

Piatus Montensis, *Praelectiones Iuris Regularis,* 3. ed., 2 vols., Tornaci, 1906.

Pichler, Vitus, *Epitome Iuris Canonici,* 2 vols., Venetiis, 1755.

Pignatelli, Jacobus, *Consultationes Canonicae,* 11 vols. in 4, Coloniae Allobrogum, 1700.

Prümmer, Dominicus, *Manuale Iuris Canonici in Usum Scholarum,* 3. ed., Friburgi Brisgoviae, 1922.

Raus, J. B., *Institutiones Canonicae iuxta Novum Codicem Iuris,* 2. ed., Parisiis: Vitte, 1931.

Reiffenstuel, Anacletus, *Ius Canonicum Universum,* 7 vols., Venetiis, 1735.

Schaefer, Timotheus, *Compenium de Religiosis ad Normam Codicis Iuris Canonici,* 2. ed., Muenster i. W.: Libr. Aschendorff, 1931.

Schmalzgrueber, Franciscus, *Ius Ecclesiasticum Universum,* 5 vols. in 12, Romae, 1843-1845.

Thomassinus, Ludovicus, *Vetus et Nova Ecclesiae Disciplina circa Beneficia et Beneficiarios,* 10 vols., Moguntiae, 1787.

Toso, Albertus, *Ad Codicem Iuris Canonici Commentaria Minora,* 5 vols., Lib. II, pars II, Romae: Jus Pontificium, 1927.

Vecchiotti, S., *Institutiones Canonicae,* 19. ed., 3 vols., Augustae Taurinorum, 1886.

Vermeersch, Arthurus, *De Religiosis Institutis et Personis,* 2 vols., Vol. I, 2. ed., Bruges, 1907.

Vermeersch, Arthurus-Creusen, Joseph, *Epitome Iuris Canonici,* 3 vols., 4. ed., Romae, Mechlinae, 1929.

Vromant, G., *De Bonis Ecclesiae Temporalibus,* Louvain: Desbarax, 1927.

Wernz, Franciscus, *Ius Decretalium ad usum Praelectionum in Scholis Textus Iuris Canonici, sive Iuris Decretalium,* 6 vols., Vol. III, 2. ed., Romae, 1908.

Wernz, Franciscus-Vidal, Petrus, *Ius Canonicum ad Codicis Normam Exactum,* 7 toms. in 8 vols., Tom. III, *De Religiosis,* Romae, Universitas Gregoriana, 1933.

Articles

Anonymous, "Maisons Religieuses,"—*Analecta Iuris Pontificii,* IV (1860), 1823 sqq.

Butler, Dom E. C., "Monasticism,"—*Cambridge Medieval History,* Vol. I, New York, 1911, pp. 521-542.

Chapman, John, "Eutyches,"—*The Catholic Encyclopedia,* V, 631-633.

Creusen, Joseph, "Fondation de Maisons Religieuses,"—*Revue des Communautés Religieuses,* XI (1935), 63-69; 97-104; 122-131.

Goyeneche, S., "Consultationes,"—*CpR,* I (1920), 114-116.

———, "Consultationes,"—*CpR.,* VII (1926), 394-396.

Jombart, E., "Les Moniales à Voeux Simples,"—*Nouvelle Revue Théologique,* LI (1924), 197 sqq.

Larraona, Arcadius, "Commentarium Codicis,"—*CpR,* I (1920), 171-177.

———, "Commentarium Codicis,"—*CpR,* II (1921), 275-287.

———, "Commentarium Codicis,"—*CpR,* III (1922), 45-53.

———, "Commentarium Codicis,"—*CpR,* V (1924), 324-334; 417-436.

Maroto, Philippus, "Annotationes,"—*CpR,* II (1921), 162-168.

———, "Annotationes,"—*CpR,* V (1924), 122-134.

Steiger, A. P., "De Propagatione et Diffusione Vitae Religiosae, Synopsis Historica,"—*Periodica,* XIII (1924), (29)-(60).

Vermeersch, Arthurus, "De Persona Morali,"—*Periodica,* X (1921), (34)-(35).

———, "Annotationes,"—*Periodica,* XIII (1924), 53-57.

———, "De Domibus Filialibus,"—*Periodica,* XVII (1928), 88*-90*.

Vromant, G., "De Licentiis Requisitis ad Erigendam Domum Religiosam,"—*Jus Pontificium,* VIII (1928), 212-215.

White, Robert, "Certain Aspects of the Legal Status of the Church in the United States,"—*The Jurist,* I (1941), 20-49.

Periodicals

Analecta Iuris Pontificii, 28 vols., Romae, 1855-1868, Paris, 1869-1891.

Commentarium pro Religiosis (later *Commentarium pro Religiosis et Missionariis*), Romae, 1920—

Jurist, The, Washington, D. C., 1941—

Jus Pontificium, Romae, 1921—

Nouvelle Revue Théologique, Paris, 1869—

Periodica de Re Canonica et Morali utili praesertim Religiosis et Missionariis, Bruges, 1905—

Revue des Communautés Religieuses, Louvain, 1925—

ABBREVIATIONS

AAS—*Acta Apostolicae Sedis.*

ASS—*Acta Sanctae Sedis.*

Bull. Roman. Taur.—*Bullarium Romanum, ed. Taurinensis.*

Coll. S. C. Ep. et Reg.—*Collectanea Sacrae Congregationis Episcoporum et Regularium.*

Coll. S. C. P. F.—*Collectanea Sacrae Congregationis de Propaganda Fide.*

CpR—*Commentarium pro Religiosis.*

Fontes—*Codicis Iuris Canonici Fontes cura—Gasparri editi.*

Mansi—*Sacrorum Conciliorum Nova et Amplissima Collectio.*

MPL—Migne, *Patrologia Latina.*

Periodica—*Periodica de Re Canonica et Morali utili praesertim Religiosis et Missionariis.*

RCR—*Revue des Communautés Religieuses.*

S. C. C.—Sacra Congregatio Concilii.

S. C. de Relig.—Sacra Congregatio de Religiosis.

S. C. Ep. et Reg.—Sacra Congregatio Episcoporum et Regularium.

S. R. C.—Sacrorum Rituum Congregatio.

S. R. R.—Sacra Romana Rota.

ANALYTICAL INDEX

BIOGRAPHICAL NOTE

Bernard Joseph Flanagan was born at Proctor, Vermont, March 31, 1908. Upon completing his studies at Proctor High School he entered Holy Cross College and received the degree of Bachelor of Arts from that institution in June, 1928. In October of the same year he entered the North American College, Rome, and attended theological classes at the University of the "Propaganda," from which he received the degree of Licentiate in Theology. He was ordained to the priesthood on December 8, 1931. At the request of his Most Reverend Bishop he entered the Graduate School of Canon Law at the Catholic University of America in the fall of 1940. He received the Baccalaureate Degree in Canon Law in June, 1941, and the Licentiate Degree in Canon Law in May, 1942.

CANON LAW STUDIES *

1. Freriks, Rev. Celestine A., C.PP.S., J.C.D., Religious Congregations in Their External Relations, 121 pp., 1916.
2. Galliher, Rev. Daniel M., O.P., J.C.D., Canonical Elections, 117 pp., 1917.
3. Borkowski, Rev. Aurelius L., O.F.M., J.C.D., De Confraternitatibus Ecclesiasticis, 136 pp., 1918.
4. Castillo, Rev. Cayo, J.C.D., Disertacion Historico-Canonica sobre la Potestad del Cabildo en Sede Vacante o Impedida del Vicario Capitular, 99 pp., 1919 (1918).
5. Kubelbeck, Rev. William J., S.T.B., J.C.D., The Sacred Penitentiaria and Its Relation to Faculties of Ordinaries and Priests, 129 pp., 1918.
6. Petrovits, Rev. Joseph, J.C., S.T.D., J.C.D., The New Church Law on Matrimony, X-461 pp., 1919.
7. Hickey, Rev. John J., S.T.B., J.C.D., Irregularities and Simple Impediments in the New Code of Canon Law, 100 pp., 1920.
8. Klekotka, Rev. Peter J., S.T.B., J.C.D., Diocesan Consultors, 179 pp., 1920.
9. Wanenmacher, Rev. Francis, J.C.D., The Evidence in Ecclesiastical Procedure Affecting the Marriage Bond, 1920 (Printed 1935).
10. Golden, Rev. Henry Francis, J.C.D., Parochial Benefices in the New Code, IV-119 pp., 1921 (Printed 1925).
11. Koudelka, Rev. Charles J., J.C.D., Pastors, Their Rights and Duties According to the New Code of Canon Law, 211 pp., 1921.
12. Melo, Rev. Antonius, O.F.M., J.C.D., De Exemptione Regularium, X-188 pp., 1921.
13. Schaaf, Rev. Valentine Theodore, O.F.M., S.T.B., J.C.D., The Cloister, X-180 pp., 1921.
14. Burke, Rev. Thomas Joseph, S.T.D., J.C.D., Competence in Ecclesiastical Tribunals, IV-117 pp., 1922.
15. Leech, Rev. George Leo, J.C.D., A Comparative Study of the Constitution "Apostolicae Sedis" and the "Codex Juris Canonici," 179 pp., 1922.
16. Motry, Rev. Hubert Louis, S.T.D., J.C.D., Diocesan Faculties According to the Code of Canon Law, II-167 pp., 1922.
17. Murphy, Rev. George Lawrence, J.C.D., Delinquencies and Penalties in the Administration and the Reception of the Sacraments, IV-121 pp., 1923.
18. O'Reilly, Rev. John Anthony, S.T.B., J.C.D., Ecclesiastical Sepulture in the New Code of Canon Law, II-129 pp., 1923.

* Below n. 100 only the following numbers are still available: Nn. 3, 4, 9, 25, 34, 57 and 75. Beginning with n. 100 only the following are unavailable: Nn. 100, 101, 102, 104, 105, 107, 108, 109, 111 and 113.

19. MICHALICKA, REV. WENCESLAS CYRILL, O.S.B., J.C.D., Judicial Procedure in Dismissal of Clerical Exempt Religious, 107 pp., 1923.
20. DARGIN, REV. EDWARD VINCENT, S.T.B., J.C.D., Reserved Cases According to the Code of Canon Law, IV-103 pp., 1924.
21. GODFREY, REV. JOHN A., S.T.B., J.C.D., The Right of Patronage According to the Code of Canon Law, 153 pp., 1924.
22. HAGEDORN, REV. FRANCIS EDWARD, J.C.D., General Legislation on Indulgences, II-154 pp., 1924.
23. KING, REV. JAMES IGNATIUS, J.C.D., The Administration of the Sacraments to Dying Non-Catholics, V-141 pp., 1924.
24. WINSLOW, REV. FRANCIS JOSEPH, O.F.M., J.C.D., Vicars and Prefects Apostolic, IV-149 pp., 1924.
25. CORREA, REV. JOSE SERVELION, S.T.L., J.C.D., La Potestad Legislativa de la Iglesia Catolica, IV-127 pp., 1925.
26. DUGAN, REV. HENRY FRANCIS, A.M., J.C.D., The Judiciary Department of the Diocesan Curia, 87 pp., 1925.
27. KELLER, REV. CHARLES FREDERICK, S.T.B., J.C.D., Mass Stipends, 167 pp., 1925.
28. PASCHANG, REV. JOHN LINUS, J.C.D., The Sacramentals According to the Code of Canon Law, 129 pp., 1925.
29. PIONTEK, REV. CYRILLUS, O.F.M., S.T.B., J.C.D., De Indulto Exclaustrationis necnon Saecularizationis, XIII-289 pp., 1925.
30. KEARNEY, REV. RICHARD JOSEPH, S.T.B., J.C.D., Sponsors at Baptism According to the Code of Canon Law, IV-127 pp., 1925.
31. BARTLETT, REV. CHESTER JOSEPH, A.M., LL.B., J.C.D., The Tenure of Parochial Property in the United States of America, V-108 pp., 1926.
32. KILKER, REV. ADRIAN JEROME, J.C.D., Extreme Unction, V-425 pp., 1926.
33. MCCORMICK, REV. ROBERT EMMETT, J.C.D., Confessors of Religious, VIII-266 pp., 1926.
34. MILLER, REV. NEWTON THOMAS, J.C.D., Founded Masses According to the Code of Canon Law, VII-93 pp., 1926.
35. ROELKER, REV. EDWARD G., S.T.D., J.C.D., Principles of Privilege According to the Code of Canon Law, XI-166 pp., 1926.
36. BAKALARCZYK, REV. RICHARDUS, M.I.C., J.U.D., De Novitiatu, VIII-208 pp., 1927.
37. PIZZUTI, REV. LAWRENCE, O.F.M., J.U.L., De Parochis Religiosis, 1927. (Not Printed.)
38. BLILEY, REV. NICHOLAS MARTIN, O.S.B., J.C.D., Altars According to the Code of Canon Law, XIX-132 pp., 1927.
39. BROWN, MR. BRENDAN FRANCIS, A.B., LL.M., J.U.D., The Canonical Juristic Personality with Special Reference to its Status in the United States of America, V-212 pp., 1927.
40. CAVANAUGH, REV. WILLIAM THOMAS, C.P., J.U.D., The Reservation of the Blessed Sacrament, VIII-101 pp., 1927.

41. Doheny, Rev. William J., C.S.C., A.B., J.U.D., Church Property: Modes of Acquisition, X-118 pp., 1927.
42. Feldhaus, Rev. Aloysius H., C.PP.S., J.C.D., Oratories, IX-141 pp., 1927.
43. Kelly, Rev. James Patrick, A.B., J.C.D., The Jurisdiction of the Simple Confessor, X-208 pp., 1927.
44. Neuberger, Rev. Nicholas J., J.C.D., Canon 6 or the Relation of the Codex Juris Canonici to the Preceding Legislation, V-95 pp., 1927.
45. O'Keefe, Rev. Gerald Michael, J.C.D., Matrimonial Dispensations, Powers of Bishops, Priests, and Confessors, VIII-232 pp., 1927.
46. Quigley, Rev. Joseph A. M., A.B., J.C.D., Condemned Societies, 139 pp., 1927.
47. Zaplotnik, Rev. Johannes Leo, J.C.D., De Vicariis Foraneis, X-142 pp., 1927.
48. Duskie, Rev. John Aloysius, A.B., J.C.D., The Canonical Status of the Orientals in the United States, VIII-196 pp., 1928.
49. Hyland, Rev. Francis Edward, J.C.D., Excommunciation, Its Nature, Historical Development and Effects, VIII-181 pp., 1928.
50. Reinmann, Rev. Gerald Joseph, O.M.C., J.C.D., The Third Order Secular of Saint Francis, 201 pp., 1928.
51. Schenk, Rev. Francis J., J.C.D., The Matrimonial Impediments of Mixed Religion and Disparity of Cult, XVI-318 pp., 1929.
52. Coady, Rev. John Joseph, S.T.D., J.U.D., A.M., The Appointment of Pastors, VIII-150 pp., 1929.
53. Kay, Rev. Thomas Henry, J.C.D., Competence in Matrimonial Procedure, VIII-164 pp., 1929.
54. Turner, Rev. Sidney Joseph, C.P., J.U.D., The Vow of Poverty, XLIX-217 pp., 1929.
55. Kearney, Rev. Raymond A., A.B., S.T.D., J.C.D., The Principles of Delegation, VII-149 pp., 1929.
56. Conran, Rev. Edward James, A.B., J.C.D., The Interdict, V-163 pp., 1930.
57. O'Neill, Rev. William H., J.C.D., Papal Rescripts of Favor, VII-218 pp., 1930.
58. Bastnagel, Rev. Clement Vincent, J.U.D., The Appointment of Parochial Adjutants and Assistants, XV-257 pp., 1930.
59. Ferry, Rev. William A., A.B., J.C.D., Stole Fees, V-136 pp., 1930.
60. Costello, Rev. John Michael, A.B., J.C.D., Domicile and Quasi-Domicile, VII-201 pp., 1930.
61. Kremer, Rev. Michael Nicholas, A.B., S.T.B., J.C.D., Church Support in the United States, VI-136 pp., 1930.
62. Angulo, Rev. Luis, C.M., J.C.D., Legislation de la Iglesia sobre la intencion en la application de la Santa Misa, VII-104 pp., 1931.
63. Frey, Rev. Wolfgang Norbert, O.S.B., A.B., J.C.D., The Act of Religious Profession, VIII-174 pp., 1931.

64. Roberts, Rev. James Brendan, A.B., J.C.D., The Banns of Marriage, XIV-140 pp., 1931.
65. Ryder, Rev. Raymond Aloysius, A.B., J.C.D., Simony, IX-151 pp., 1931.
66. Campagna, Rev. Angelo, Ph.D., J.U.D., Il Vicario Generale del Vescovo, VII-205 pp., 1931.
67. Cox, Rev. Joseph Godfrey, A.B., J.C.D., The Administration of Seminaries, VI-124 pp., 1931.
68. Gregory, Rev. Donald J., J.U.D., The Pauline Privilege, XV-165 pp., 1931.
69. Donohue, Rev. John F., J.C.D., The Impediment of Crime, VII-110 pp., 1931.
70. Dooley, Rev. Eugene A., O.M.I., J.C.D., Church Law on Sacred Relics, IX-143 pp., 1931.
71. Orth, Rev. Clement Raymond, O.M.C., J.C.D., The Approbation of Religious Institutes, 171 pp., 1931.
72. Pernicone, Rev. Joseph M., A.B., J.C.D., The Ecclesiastical Prohibition of Books, XII-267 pp., 1932.
73. Clinton, Rev. Connell, A.B., J.C.D., The Paschal Precept, IX-108 pp., 1932.
74. Donnelly, Rev. Francis B., A.M., S.T.L., J.C.D., The Diocesan Synod, VIII-125 pp., 1932.
75. Torrente, Rev. Camilo, C.M.F., J.C.D., Las Processiones Sagradas, V-145 pp., 1932.
76. Murphy, Rev. Edwin J., C.PP.S., J.C.D., Suspension Ex Informata Conscientia, XI-122 pp., 1932.
77. MacKenzie, Rev. Eric F., A.M., S.T.L., J.C.D., The Delict of Heresy in its Commission, Penalization, Absolution, VII-124 pp., 1932.
78. Lyons, Rev. Avitus E., S.T.B., J.C.D., The Collegiate Tribunal of First Instance, XI-147 pp., 1932.
79. Connolly, Rev. Thomas A., J.C.D., Appeals, XI-195 pp., 1932.
80. Sangmeister, Rev. Joseph V., A.B., J.C.D., Force and Fear as Precluding Matrimonial Consent, V-211 pp., 1932.
81. Jaeger, Rev. Leo A., A.B., J.C.D., The Administration of Vacant and Quasi-Vacant Episcopal Sees in the United States, IX-229 pp., 1932.
82. Rimlinger, Rev. Herbert T., J.C.D., Error Invalidating Matrimonial Consent, VII-79 pp., 1932.
83. Barrett, Rev. John D. M., S.S., J.C.D., A Comparative Study of the Third Plenary Council of Baltimore and the Code, IX-221 pp., 1932.
84. Carberry, Rev. John J., Ph.D., S.T.D., J.C.D., The Juridical Form of Marriage, X-177 pp., 1934.
85. Dolan, Rev. John L., A.B., J.C.D., The Defensor Vinculi, XII-157 pp., 1934.
86. Hannan, Rev. Jerome D., A.M., S.T.D., LL.B., J.C.D., The Canon Law of Wills, IX-517 pp., 1934.

87. Lemieux, Rev. Delise A., A.M., J.C.D., The Sentence in Ecclesiastical Procedure, IX-131 pp., 1934.
88. O'Rourke, Rev. James J., A.B., J.C.D., Parish Registers, VII-109 pp., 1934.
89. Timlin, Rev. Bartholomew, O.F.M., A.M., J.C.D., Conditional Matrimonial Consent, X-381 pp., 1934.
90. Wahl, Rev. Francis X., A.B., J.C.D., The Matrimonial Impediments of Consanguinity and Affinity, VI-125 pp., 1934.
91. White, Rev. Robert J., A.B., LL.B., S.T.B., J.C.D., Canonical Ante-Nuptial Promises and the Civil Law, VI-152 pp., 1934.
92. Herrera, Rev. Antonio Parra, O.C.D., J.C.D., Legislacion Ecclesiastica sobra el Ayuno y la Abstinencia, XI-191 pp., 1935.
93. Kennedy, Rev. Edwin J., J.C.D., The Special Matrimonial Process in Cases of Evident Nullity, X-165 pp., 1935.
94. Manning, Rev. John J., A.B., J.C.D., Presumption of Law in Matrimonial Procedure, XI-111 pp., 1935.
95. Moeder, Rev. John M., J.C.D., The Proper Bishop for Ordination and Dimissorial Letters, VII-135 pp., 1935.
96. O'Mara, Rev. William A., A.B., J.C.D., Canonical Causes for Matrimonial Dispensations, IX-155 pp., 1935.
97. Reilly, Rev. Peter, J.C.D., Residence of Pastors, IX-81 pp., 1935.
98. Smith, Rev. Mariner T., O.P., S.T.Lr., J.C.D., The Penal Law for Religious, VII-169 pp., 1935.
99. Whalen, Rev. Donald W., A.M., J.C.D., The Value of Testimonial Evidence in Matrimonial Procedure, XIII-297 pp., 1935.
100. Cleary, Rev. Joseph F., J.C.D., Canonical Limitations on the Alienation of Church Property, VIII-141 pp., 1936.
101. Glynn, Rev. John C., J.C.D., The Promoter of Justice, XX-337 pp., 1936.
102. Brennan, Rev. James H., S.S., M.A., S.T.B., J.C.D., The Simple Convalidation of Marriage, VI-135 pp., 1937.
103. Brunini, Rev. Joseph Bernard, J.C.D., The Clerical Obligations of Canons 139 and 142, X-121 pp., 1937.
104. Connor, Rev. Maurice, A.B., J.C.D., The Administrative Removal of Pastors, VIII-159 pp., 1937.
105. Guilfoyle, Rev. Merlin Joseph, J.C.D., Custom, XI-144 pp., 1937.
106. Hughes, Rev. James Austin, A.B., A.M., J.C.D., Witnesses in Criminal Trials of Clerics, IX-140 pp., 1937.
107. Jansen, Rev. Raymond J., A.B., S.T.L., J.C.D., Canonical Provisions for Catechetical Instruction, VII-153 pp., 1937.
108. Kealy, Rev. John James, A.B., J.C.D., The Introductory Libellus in Church Court Procedure, XI-121 pp., 1937.
109. McManus, Rev. James Edward, C.SS.R., J.C.D., The Administration of Temporal Goods in Religious Institutes, XVI-196 pp., 1937.

110. MORIARTY, REV. EUGENE JAMES, J.C.D., Oaths in Ecclesiastical Courts, X-115 pp., 1937.

111. RAINER, REV. ELIGIUS GEORGE, C.SS.R., J.C.D., Suspension of Clerics, XVII-249 pp., 1937.

112. REILLY, REV. THOMAS F., C.SS.R., J.C.D., Visitation of Religious, VI-195 pp., 1938.

113. MORIARTY, REV. FRANCIS E., C.SS.R., J.C.D., The Extraordinary Absolution from Censures, XV-334 pp., 1938.

114. CONNOLLY, REV. NICHOLAS P., J.C.D., The Canonical Erection of Parishes, X-132 pp., 1938.

115. DONOVAN, REV. JAMES JOSEPH, J.C.D., The Pastor's Obligation in Prenuptial Investigation, XII-322 pp., 1938.

116. HARRIGAN, REV. ROBERT J., M.A., S.T.B., J.C.D., The Radical Sanation of Invalid Marriages, VIII-208 pp., 1938.

117. BOFFA, REV. CONRAD HUMBERT, J.C.D., Canonical Provisions for Catholic Schools, VII-211 pp., 1939.

118. PARSONS, REV. ANSCAR JOHN, O.M.Cap., J.C.D., Canonical Elections, XII-236 pp., 1939.

119. REILLY, REV. EDWARD MICHAEL, A.B., J.C.D., The General Norms of Dispensation, XII-156 pp., 1939.

120. RYAN, REV. GERALD ALOYSIUS, A.B., J.C.D., Principles of Episcopal Jurisdiction, XII-172 pp., 1939.

121. BURTON, REV. FRANCIS JAMES, C.S.C., A.B., J.C.D., A Commentary on Canon 1125, X-222 pp., 1940.

122. MIASKIEWICZ, REV. FRANCIS SIGISMUND, J.C.D., Supplied Jurisdiction According to Canon 209, XII-340 pp., 1940.

123. RICE, REV. PATRICK WILLIAM, A.B., J.C.D., Proof of Death in Prenuptial Investigation, VIII-156 pp., 1940.

124. ANGLIN, REV. THOMAS FRANCIS, M.S., J.C.D., The Eucharistic Fast, VIII-183 pp., 1941.

125. COLEMAN, REV. JOHN JEROME, J.C.D., The Minister of Confirmation, VI-153 pp., 1941.

126. DOWNS, REV. JOSEPH EMMANUEL, A.B., J.C.D., The Concept of Clerical Immunity, XI-163 pp., 1941.

127. ESSWEIN, REV. ANTHONY ALBERT, J.C.D., Extrajudicial Penal Powers of Ecclesiastical Superiors, X-144 pp., 1941.

128. FARRELL, REV. BENJAMIN FRANCIS, M.A., S.T.L., J.C.D., The Rights and Duties of the Local Ordinary Regarding Congregations of Women Religious of Pontifical Approval, V-195 pp., 1941.

129. FEENEY, REV. THOMAS JOHN, A.B., S.T.L., J.C.D., Restitutio in Integrum, VI-169 pp., 1941.

130. FINDLAY, REV. STEPHEN WILLIAM, O.S.B., A.B., J.C.D., Canonical Norms Governing the Deposition and Degradation of Clerics, XVII-279 pp., 1941.

131. Goodwine, Rev. John, A.B., S.T.L., J.C.D., The Right of the Church to Acquire Property, VIII-119 pp., 1941.
132. Heston, Rev. Edward Louis, C.S.C., Ph.D., S.T.D., J.C.D., The Alienation of Church Property in the United States, XII-222 pp., 1941.
133. Hogan, Rev. James John, A.B., S.T.L., J.C.D., Judicial Advocates and Procurators, XIII-200 pp., 1941.
134. Kealy, Rev. Thomas M., A.B., Litt.B., J.C.D., Dowry of Women Religious, IX-152 pp., 1941.
135. Keene, Rev. Michael James, O.S.B., J.C.D., Religious Ordinaries and Canon 198, V-164 pp., 1942.
136. Kerin, Rev. Charles A., S.S., M.A., S.T.B., J.C.D., The Privation of Christian Burial, XVI-279 pp., 1941.
137. Louis, Rev. William Francis, M.A., J.C.D., Diocesan Archives, X-101 pp., 1941.
138. McDevitt, Rev. Gilbert Joseph, A.B., J.C.D., Legitimacy and Legitimation, X-247 pp., 1941.
139. McDonough, Rev. Thomas Joseph, A.B., J.C.D., Apostolic Administrators, X-217 pp., 1941.
140. Meier, Rev. Carl Anthony, A.B., J.C.D., Penal Administration Procedure Against Negligent Pastors, XI-240 pp., 1941.
141. Schmidt, Rev. John Rogg, A.B., J.C.D., The Principles of Authentic Interpretation in Canon 17 of the Code of Canon Law, XII-331 pp., 1941.
142. Slafkosky, Rev. Andrew Leonard, A.B., J.C.D., The Canonical Episcopal Visitation of the Diocese, X-197 pp., 1941.
143. Swoboda, Rev. Innocent Robert, O.F.M., J.C.D., Ignorance in Relation to the Imputability of Delicts, IX-271 pp., 1941.
144. Dubé, Rev. Arthur Joseph, A.B., J.C.D., The General Principles for the Reckoning of Time in Canon Law, VIII-299 pp., 1941.
145. McBride, Rev. James T., A.B., J.C.D., Incardination and Excardination of Seculars, XX-585 pp., 1941.
146. Król, Rev. John T., J.C.D., The Defendant in Ecclesiastical Trials, XII-207 pp., 1942.
147. Comyns, Rev. Joseph J., C.SS.R., A.B., J.C.D., Papal and Episcopal Administration of Church Property, XIV-155 pp., 1942.
148. Barry, Rev. Garrett Francis, O.M.I., J.J.D., Violation of the Cloister, XII-260 pp,, 1942.
149. Bolduc, Rev. Gatien, C.S.V., A.B., S.T.L., J.C.D., Les Études dans les Religions Cléricales, VIII-155 pp., 1942.
150. Boyle, Rev. David John, M.A., J.C.D., The Juridic Effects of Moral Certitude on Pre-Nuptial Guarantees, XII-188 pp., 1942.
151. Canavan, Rev. Walter Joseph, M.A., Litt.D., J.C.D., The Profession of Faith, XII-143 pp., 1942.
152. Desrochers, Rev. Bruno, A.B., Ph.L., S.T.B., J.C.D., Le Premier Concile Plénier de Québec et le Code de Droit Canonique, XIV-186 pp., 1942.

153. DILLON, REV. ROBERT EDWARD, A.B., J.C.D., Common Law Marriage, X-148 pp., 1942.
154. DODWELL, REV. EDWARD JOHN, PH.D., S.T.B., J.C.L., The Time and Place for the Celebration of Marriage.
155. DONNELLAN, REV. THOMAS ANDREW, A.B., J.C.D., The Obligation of the Missa pro Populo, VII-131 pp., 1942.
156. ELTZ, REV. LOUIS ANTHONY, A.B., J.C.L., Cooperation in Crime.
157. GASS, REV. SYLVESTER FRANCIS, M.A., J.C.L., Ecclesiastical Pensions, XI-206 pp., 1942.
158. GUINIVEN, REV. JOHN JOSEPH, C.SS.R., J.C.D., The Precept of Hearing Mass, XIV-188 pp., 1942.
159. GULCZYNSKI, REV. JOHN THEOPHILUS, J.C.L., The Desecration and Violation of Churches.
160. HAMMILL, REV. JOHN LEO, M.A., J.C.D., The Obligations of the Traveler According to Canon 14, VIII-204 pp., 1942.
161. HAYDT, REV. JOHN JOSEPH, A.B., J.C.D., Reserved Benefices, XI-148 pp., 1942.
162. HUSER, REV. ROGER JOHN, O.F.M., A.B., J.C.L., The Crime of Abortion in Canon Law.
163. KEARNEY, REV. FRANCIS PATRICK, A.B., S.T.L., J.C.L., The Principles of Canon 1127.
164. LINAHEN, REV. LEO JAMES, S.T.L., J.C.D., De Absolutione Complicis In Peccato Turpi, 114 pp., 1942.
165. MCCLOSKEY, REV. JOSEPH ALOYSIUS, A.B., J.C.D., The Subject of Ecclesiastical Law According to Canon 12, XVII-246 pp., 1942.
166. O'NEILL, REV. FRANCIS JOSEPH, C.SS.R., J.C.D., The Dismissal of Religious in Temporary Vows, XIII-220 pp., 1942.
167. PRINCE, REV. JOHN EDWARD, A.B., S.T.B., J.C.D., The Diocesan Chancellor, X-136 pp., 1942.
168. RIESNER, REV. ALBERT JOSEPH, C.SS.R., J.C.D., Apostates and Fugitives from Religious Institutes, IX-168 pp., 1942.
169. STENGER, REV. JOSEPH BERNARD, J.C.D., The Mortgaging of Church Property, 186 pp., 1942.
170. WALDRON, REV. JOSEPH FRANCIS, A.B., J.C.D., The Minister of Baptism, XII-197 pp., 1942.
171. WILLETT, REV. ROBERT ALBERT, J.C.D., The Probative Value of Documents in Ecclesiastical Trials, X-124 pp., 1942.
172. WOEBER, REV. EDWARD MARTIN, M.A., J.C.D., The Interpellations, XII-161 pp., 1942.
173. BENKO, REV. MATTHEW ALOYSIUS, O.S.B., M.A., J.C.L., The Abbot *Nullius*.
174. CHRIST, REV. JOSEPH JAMES, M.A., S.T.L., J.C.L., Dispensation from Vindicative Penalties.
175. CLANCY, REV. PATRICK M. J., O.P., A.B., S.T.LR., J.C.L., The Local Religious Superior.

176. Clarke, Rev. Thomas James, J.C.L., Parish Societies.
177. Connolly, Rev. John Patrick, S.T.L., J.C.L., Synodal Examiners and Parish Priest Consultors.
178. Drumm, Rev. William Martin, A.B., J.C.L., Hospital Chaplains.
179. Flanagan, Rev. Bernard Joseph, A.B., S.T.L., J.C.L., The Canonical Erection of Religious Houses.
180. Kelleher, Rev. Stephen Joseph, A.B., S.T.B., J.C.L., Discussions with non-Catholics: Canonical Legislation.
181. Lewis, Rev. Gordian, C.P., J.C.L., Chapters in Religious Institutes.
182. Marx, Rev. Adolph, J.C.L., The Declaration of Nullity of Marriages Contracted Outside the Church.
183. Matulenas, Rev. Raymond Anthony, O.S.B., A.B., J.C.L., Communication, a Source of Privileges.
184. O'Leary, Rev. Charles Gerard, C.SS.R., Religious Dismissed After Perpetual Profession.
185. Power, Rev. Cornelius Michael, J.C.L., The Blessing of Cemeteries.
186. Shuhler, Rev. Ralph Vincent, O.S.A., J.C.L., Privileges of Religious to Absolve and Dispense.
187. Ziolkowski, Rev. Thaddeus Stanislaus, A.B., J.C.L., The Consecration and Blessing of Churches.

www.ingramcontent.com/pod-product-compliance
Lightning Source LLC
LaVergne TN
LVHW050219080826
844660LV00012B/438

* 9 7 8 0 8 1 3 2 2 3 6 8 1 *